THE RHYTHMS
OF TONAL MUSIC

JOEL LESTER

SOUTHERN ILLINOIS UNIVERSITY PRESS
Carbondale and Edwardsville

Library of Congress Cataloging-in-Publication Data

Lester, Joel.
  The rhythms of tonal music.

  Includes index.
  1. Musical meter and rhythm—Addresses, essays,
lectures.   2. Musical analysis.   I. Title.
  MT42.L48   1986   781.6'2   85-22293
  ISBN 0-8093-1282-4

    90 89 88 87 86   5 4 3 2 1

For examples 5-12 and 5-13 (Schoenberg, *Chamber Symphony,* op. 9): Used by permission of Belmont Music Publishers. Copyright 1912 by Universal Edition, AG.

For examples 7-9 and 7-10 (examples from Arthur Komar, *A Theory of Suspensions*): Used by permission of Peer Publications. Copyright 1971 by Princeton University Press.

For example 7-11 (example from Peter Westergaard, *An Introduction to Tonal Theory*): Reproduced from *An Introduction to Tonal Theory* by Peter Westergaard, by permission of W. W. Norton & Company, Inc. Copyright © 1975 by W. W. Norton & Company, Inc.

For examples 6-1, 6-2, 6-6, 6-15, 7-2, 7-3, 7-4, and 9-7 (examples from Heinrich Schenker, *Free Composition*): Reprinted with permission of Schirmer Books, a Division of Macmillan, Inc. from Heinrich Schenker, *Free Composition,* translated and edited by Ernst Oster. Copyright 1935, 1956 by Universal Edition, AG. Translation, Copyright © 1979 by Schirmer Books.

CONTENTS

v

PREFACE

Our generation is witness to a profusion of books, articles, and dissertations on rhythm. As the author of each study has built upon the research of earlier writings, an increasingly sophisticated awareness of many aspects of rhythm has arisen. Many of these studies focus primarily on one or two aspects of rhythm: grouping, accent, hypermeter, rhythms of textural components, rhythm and linear analysis, phrase rhythm, continuity, musical form, rhythm and performance, and so forth. I believe that what is needed at this time is a more comprehensive work, one that reviews the available literature and that can bring to the individual facets of rhythm the benefits of a larger perspective.

The present book attempts such a comprehensive study. But it is by no means only a survey of existing literature. A new approach to the treatment of accent (presented in chapter 2) directly affects the understanding of meter and, by extension, provides a new way of approaching the issues of hypermeter, phrase rhythm, rhythm and style, and rhythm and texture; it also plays a major role in the evaluation of recent studies that relate rhythm to linear analysis. The discussion of rhythm and form is also without precedent in the literature on rhythm.

It is my hope that by surveying our present knowledge, by building on the already considerable knowledge shared by the various existing studies, and by raising more issues than can possibly be answered, *The Rhythms of Tonal Music* will demonstrate and enhance the considerable current state of our knowledge of the working of musical rhythm and will act as a spur to further research.

This study limits itself to rhythm in tonal music for several reasons. Pitch structuring is an important aspect of rhythm in any music. Only in tonal music is there a basic pitch syntax common to all compositions. And despite doctrinal differences, only in the realm of tonal music do most musicians generally agree on how pitch is structured. To have included pretonal and posttonal music would have meant extensive digressions arguing and defending assertions of pitch structure in this music, diluting the concentration on rhythm. Many approaches discussed in this book can be applied to pretonal and posttonal music as well. But no attempt has been made to do so here.

In an area of study so filled with ideas and insights, it is often difficult to know whether a given idea is original, is taken from an earlier, only half-remembered article, book, or conversation, or is an amalgam of ideas presented in several separate studies. I have made every attempt to credit the sources of those citations that I can trace. I apologize in advance for the references I might have omitted. There is also no way I can ever trace to their source the many ideas that arose during three doctoral seminars I conducted on rhythm during the past eight years—one at the Eastman School of Music, the remaining two at the Graduate Center of the City University of New York. My thanks to all the students involved for their ever-illuminating critiques and their forebearance and accurate aim whenever I floated trial balloons that needed rapid deflating. My thanks also to the City College of New York for the sabbatical leave in the spring of 1984, without which this book might never have been completed. And finally, my thanks to Robert Phillips, Dan Gunter, and Yvonne Mattson of SIU Press for their interest in this work and their untiring attention to crucial details. Without their care this book could not have appeared in its present form.

THE RHYTHMS
OF TONAL MUSIC

1

THE STUDY OF RHYTHM

MUSIC IN TIME AND MUSIC NOTATION

Music can exist only in time. From such fundamentals as the differentiation of pitches from one another and the distinction between melody and harmony to the whole range of musical interactions (including but not limited to harmonic succession, melodic structure, texture, phrasing, form, climax, and even style), time is of critical importance. The difference between one pitch and another depends on the rate of vibration per unit of time. Melody arises from pitches following one another in time, harmony from pitches sounding simultaneously. Functional tonality arises from particular orderings of harmonies interacting with particular melodies. Musical form, from motives to phrasing to the largest subdivisions of a piece, is the division of a piece into segments following one another in time as they add up to the whole. The processes of growth and decline, antecedence and consequence, preparation and resolution, and motion toward and recession from climax, regardless of how they are described and in whatever terms, all depend on orderings of musical elements and relationships in time.

Performances of a piece of music and perception of that performance are possible only as they occur in time. As performers or listeners we create (or re-create, as the case may be) the piece in chronological order, one instant at a time. When we look at a painting, a sculpture, an object, or an architectural structure, we can stand back and view the work of art as a whole, but we cannot physically distance ourselves from a piece of music so as to take in all at once an entire musical work or even a small portion of that work. A pair of melodic pitches, or even the beginning and end of a single pitch, can only be perceived successively, not synoptically.

In the types of stationary art works just enumerated, the

1

shapes, colors, and textures of the art work may predispose us toward a particular mode, order, or even pace of viewing. But the manner of viewing remains an option of the viewer. We may begin from a distance with a synoptic overview and move closer to see the details in any of an infinite number of orderings. Or we may begin by lingering on details in any of these orderings and only then stand back to view the whole. Our field of vision may move among adjacent areas, or it may flit from one side to another, juxtaposing areas not physically adjacent in the art work. On any given viewing of the work—any "performance" of the work, as Cone so aptly describes it[1]—we may stand close to study details successively. Or we may repeatedly shift our perspective from details to the larger field within which these details exist. On any single viewing of the art work, we may include the entire work, many portions of that work, or only a few sections. Repeated viewings of the work, or simultaneous viewings by different persons, will almost certainly result in different performances.

In the domain of music, such freedom of choice in the order and the pacing of perception is inconceivable. The very notion of a melody, a harmony, and even a tonality would disappear if the pitches or sections of a piece could be heard in any order that the listener chose. Among the visual arts, only those art forms that occur in time, such as film, theater, or dance, are analogous to music in terms of performance in time. The ordering and the pacing of the frames of a film are as essential to its presentation and perception as the ordering and pacing of the elements are in a piece of music.

A rather extreme demonstration of the difference between our mode of hearing a piece of music and our mode of viewing a stationary work of art arises if we switch the modes of perception from one category of artform to the other—if we view an art work one iota at a time, or if we hear a piece of music as a totality all at once. Imagine that we would approach a large painting with an opaque sheet of paper containing an aperture one inch square and that we would proceed to view the entire painting by exposing it one square inch at a time—reserving only for our imagination and memory the manner in which these fragments add up to the whole. Or imagine that we would view a coarse-grained photograph (such as those printed in newspapers) through a microscope, one speck at a time—again reserving only for our memory and imagination the construction of the whole.

We may at first consider it absurd to hear music synoptically,

2

rather than chronologically. After all, where is there a "time-space" in which we can "stand back" and perceive an entire phrase as one unit without having to hear its constituent parts one by one in order? Such synoptic perception of heard music may well be impossible. But music notation, as a visual representation of some aspects of heard music, lends itself easily to synoptic perception. We can look at a musical phrase as a whole or grasp at once the shape of a melody. Indeed, we can view a single note, no matter its duration, as a single symbol, ignoring its separate beginning, continuation, and termination in heard music.

To be sure, we are usually aware that music occurs in time. Yet the ease of dealing with the fixed and verifiable symbols of music notation rather than with the intangible and fleeting sounds of heard music often seduces us in our analyses into accepting the notation of a sound as a representation of our perception of that sound. Assuming that the notation fully represents the heard music can lead to facile solutions that agree with our visual perception of the notation but not necessarily with our aural perception of the heard music. Opportunities arise in the course of this book to observe this phenomenon. One single instance suffices at this point.

It is generally recognized that in the context of shorter durations, we perceive a longer duration as accented. Such accents are perceived on the attack of the note. So in a rhythm such as that of example 1-1, each half note is accented. That each notated half note is longer than the quarters that precede and follow is obvious at a glance. But if we hear the rhythm, at what point are we aware that the half notes are longer than the quarters? Surely not at the instant of their attack. We can only know that the half notes are longer than the quarters after their midpoints are past. But if we do not know that the half notes are longer than the quarter notes until after their midpoints, how can we perceive the half notes as accented at their beginnings?

1–1

Clearly, the perception of accents caused by relative length involves factors in addition to the actual length of the note—factors such as an expectation of the length of the note before that note is actually heard based on knowledge of the passage, predictable patterns in the passage, and so forth. In this, as in many other issues that this book touches upon, viewing the notated symbols synoptically as fully representative of our perception of the heard passage can prevent us from confronting crucial aspects of those issues in the music we hear. As Charles Smith succinctly states, there are significant differences between "music-as-sound, music-as-notated-object, and music-as-cognitive-entity."[2]

THE STUDY OF RHYTHM

The intimate relationship between time and virtually all aspects of music causes the study of almost any musical aspect to be in some sense the study of rhythm. Just as it is impossible to discuss most musical aspects without considering rhythm, at least implicitly, it is impossible to discuss rhythm in isolation from other musical aspects. The choice of which aspects to emphasize affects the tone of the discussion and even the definition of basic terms.

The theoretical literature of the past generation treats a wide range of rhythmic issues. Grosvenor Cooper and Leonard Meyer's joint study *The Rhythmic Structure of Music*[3] concentrates on the musical application of prosody-based accentual patterns on levels ranging from note-to-note connections to entire movements. Edward Cone's *Musical Form and Musical Performance*[4] considers phrase rhythm and the relationship of rhythmic hierarchies to musical style. Arthur Komar's *Theory of Suspensions*,[5] Maury Yeston's *Stratification of Musical Rhythm*,[6] Peter Westergaard's *Introduction to Tonal Theory*,[7] and Carl Schachter's articles on rhythm[8] all consider, with rather different methodologies and conclusions, the relationships between layered pitch structures (Schenkerian structures) and rhythmic levels, among other issues. Komar, Westergaard, and Schachter treat phrase rhythm; Komar, Schachter, Westergaard, and Yeston explore the nature of meter; and Westergaard considers some aspects of the perception of rhythm and meter. Wallace Berry's *Structural Functions in Music*[9] discusses in depth several aspects of rhythm, among them phrase rhythm and the rhythms of various musical processes other than immediate note-to-note rhythms. John Graziano's unpublished dissertation, "A Theory of Accent in Tonal Music of the Classic-Romantic Period,"[10] is a study of the nature of accent. Reviews of these books and articles of differing length treat these and other issues.

In pursuit of these studies, some authors have defined rhythm broadly and then acknowledged that their focus is a particular area of musical rhythm, while others have redefined the very term *rhythm* to match their own focus. At one end of the spectrum lie definitions by Berry and Boretz. Berry's definition of rhythm is as broad as his field of inquiry: "All element-processes are rhythmic. In an important sense, the study of rhythm is thus the study of all musical elements, the actions of those elements producing the effects of pace, pattern, and grouping which constitute rhythm."[11] For Benjamin Boretz, rhythm is the universal aspect of music: . . . "the *rhythmic* structure of a piece is . . . simply all of its *musical* structure, subsuming every dimensional and interdimensional substructure, *including* as a more or less significant aspect the foreground substructure of attack durations. The theory of rhythm, then, is nothing more or less than the theory of musical structure in its most comprehensive form."[12]

At the other end of the spectrum lies Cooper and Meyer's rather narrow definition of rhythm, a definition that proceeds from their contention that accents on any given structural level are focal points attracting any unaccented preceding or consequent events. For them, the groupings that arise from this organizational power of accounts are themselves musical rhythm. "Rhythm may be defined as the way in which one or more unaccented beats are grouped in relation to an accented one."[13] Grouping is certainly an aspect of musical rhythm, but surely neither the only such aspect nor necessarily the most important one.

I prefer to follow Berry's example and define the term *rhythm* as broadly as possible before proceeding to the diverse aspects of rhythm. In this book, the term *rhythm* in its generic sense refers to the durational aspect of music. In this meaning, rhythm joins pitch (melody and harmony) as a primary element of music. Within this broad area the following aspects of musical rhythm may be identified:

I. Durational patterns
    A. of individual parts (the rhythm of a part)
    B. of textures (composite rhythm)
    C. of changes in
        1. harmony (harmonic rhythm or rhythm of harmonic change)
        2. texture
        3. timbre

> 4. articulation
> 5. dynamics
> 6. other aspects

II. Accent and Meter
    A. of note-to-note and measure-to-measure
    B. of larger levels
        1. phrase accentuation and hypermeter
        2. accent, meter, and musical form
III. Grouping or segmentation (motives, phrasing, form)
IV. Musical continuity and flow

Durational Patterns

Durational patterns are perhaps what is most commonly brought to mind by the term *rhythm*. Indeed, the term is commonly used to denote such a pattern. We are perhaps most familiar with the durational pattern of single melodies or of a single part in a texture. In Bach's *Fugue in C Minor* (*Well-Tempered Clavier*, I), for instance, the durational pattern of the subject is that in example 1-2.

1–2. Bach, *Fugue in C Minor* (*Well-Tempered Clavier*, I)

In addition, durational patterns of musical elements other than single parts in a texture are often important. The term *composite rhythm* refers to the durational pattern of all parts in a texture. In example 1-3, again from Bach's *C-Minor Fugue*, the composite rhythm of measures 3–4 is close to the rhythm of the fugue subject itself. But the composite rhythm of measures 5–6 is neither expressed nor approximated by any single part in the texture. For much of this fugue, the composite rhythm during statements of the fugue subject is that in measures 3–4, while nearly all passages that do not present the complete fugue subject feature a composite rhythm of continuous sixteenth notes (as in measures 5–6 of example 1-3).

    Composite rhythm thus not only affects rhythmic continuity, but also bears on form. Changes in composite rhythm can help articulate sectional divisions. This occurs in tonal music of all histori-

1–3. Bach, *Fugue in C Minor* (*Well-Tempered Clavier*, I)

cal eras. In addition to the Bach *C-Minor Fugue* (in which the absence of continuous sixteenths during subject appearances sets off these sections from the episodes) see the first movement of Beethoven's *Piano Sonata,* op. 90, in which the very opening material avoids any notes on the second beat of the measure, while the second theme group features a prominent second beat in virtually every measure; in the first movement of Brahms' *Fourth Symphony,* op. 98, the composite rhythm of the first theme group features steady eighths almost throughout, while the second theme group opens with material that avoids continuous eighths and includes many quarter-note triplets.

In other passages, an unchanging composite rhythm may create continuity across sectional divisions, emphasizing larger continuities. Think of the continuous eighths that proceed from the end of the development into the recapitulation in the first movement of Beethoven's "Appassionata" *Piano Sonata,* op. 57 (measures 134ff.). Tchaikovsky's *Romeo and Juliet* draws upon continuities in the composite rhythm to create a single dramatic sweep through much of the recapitulation, contrasting with the separate sections of the exposition, each of which has its own rhythmic profile. (Compare measures 364–417 to measures 160–271.)

Changes in composite rhythm may articulate sectional divisions entirely different from those created by other factors. The slow movement of Beethoven's "Pathétique" *Piano Sonata,* op. 13, for instance, is a five-part rondo: A (measures 1–16), B (17–28), A (29–36), C (37–50), A (51–66), coda (67–73). The change in the composite rhythm from continuous sixteenths to continuous six-

7

teenth triplets divides the movement quite differently into two nearly equal portions (1–36, 37–73).

Gradual changes in composite rhythm contribute powerfully to increases or decreases in the overall level of activity in a section, often supporting changes in other facets. The role of composite rhythm in shaping toward or away from points of climax or arrival is discussed in detail in chapter 8 ("Rhythm and Form").

Composite rhythm also plays an important role in stylistic differentiation. The motor rhythms of much music of the high Baroque and the maintenance of a single rhythmic profile for long passages in much nineteenth-century music stand in contrast to the more varied rhythms of much Classical music.

The durational pattern of harmonic change, sometimes called *harmonic rhythm* or the *rhythm of harmonic change,* is usually a crucial factor in establishing our perception of meter in tonal music, a factor to be discussed in depth in chapter 3. In addition, changes of pace in the harmonic rhythm often signal important events in a piece, such as the cadence to a phrase or section, the beginning of a new section, or increases or decreases in the general level of activity. Example 1-4 presents the first theme group and beginning of the

1–4. Haydn, *Piano Sonata,* Hob. XVI/29, first movement

transition from the first movement of Haydn's *Piano Sonata in F* (Hob. XVI/29). The cadential progressions in measures 4–5 and in measure 6 feature a sudden increase in the rate of harmonic change. The music following measure 6 differs from the preceding music not only in motive, texture, and register but also in durational pattern (the introduction of continuous sixteenths) and harmonic rhythm.

The durational patterns of *textural or timbral change* are often critical in delineating formal shapes on a variety of levels. Listen to example 1-5 from the opening of Mozart's *Piano Sonata*, K. 283. The increasing pace of harmonic changes and textural changes as the phrase progresses complements the more active melodic rhythm and the increasing range of the melody in creating the dramatic growth of the phrase.

In the excerpt from Tchaikovsky's *Symphony No. 4* in example 1-6, the increasing pace of timbral changes is perhaps the crucial factor in continuing the growth of activity after the dynamics have reached their peak.

The durational patterns of any measurable aspect can and do function like textural and timbral changes in many tonal pieces. These aspects include, but are not limited to, changes in dynamics and mode of articulation.

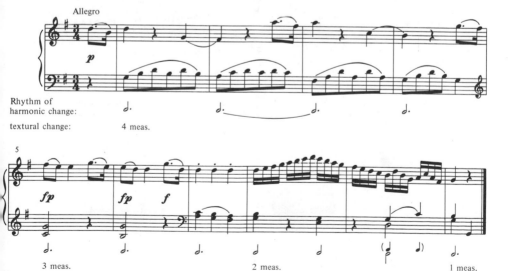

1–5. Mozart, *Piano Sonata*, K. 283, first movement

1–6. Tchaikovsky, *Symphony No. 4,* op. 36, first movement

1–6. *(Continued)*

Durational patterns, whether in a single part, in the composite rhythm, in the harmonic rhythm, or in any other factor, bear directly on the levels of activity we perceive, both in terms of tempo and in the activity within a given tempo. Because the interaction of all these durational patterns is different in every piece of music, as well as in different passages within a given piece, we can perceive such a variety of pacings in music even when the metronome markings are constant. Several later chapters examine levels of activity in detail.[14]

Accent and Meter

Accent is another primary aspect of rhythm. The term accent refers to the relative strength of a note or other musical event in relation to surrounding notes or events. The wide range of factors that give rise to our perception of accent is discussed in chapter 2, along with the effects of accent on various aspects of music and on our perception of music.

Meter, one type of accentuation, is of course a crucial aspect of rhythm in tonal music and is discussed extensively in chapter 3.

Grouping or Segmentation

There has been considerable discussion in recent decades concerning whether metric accentuation and other types of accent affect only the immediate note-to-note and measure-to-measure continuity of music or whether these accentuations also operate over larger spans of music. Even among those who accept the notion of metric and other accents on higher levels of structure, there is disagreement concerning the nature of such accents, the factors that give rise to them, and their placement. Such issues concern phrase structure and musical form, which, in turn, are part of the larger concept of *grouping* or *segmentation*—a third primary aspect of rhythm. Grouping, or segmentation, refers to the division of musical continuity into separate sections on a variety of levels ranging from individual motives to sections of movements.

Musical Continuity

Finally, rhythm is a study not only of divisions of musical time (into durational patterns, accentuations, and groupings) but also of *musical continuity*—of those factors that give rise to the vitality of music as it flows from one instant to the next. Discussions of issues throughout this book illuminate the ways in which these factors create musical vitality.

The interaction of all these aspects of rhythm—durational patterns, accent and meter, grouping or segmentation, and musical continuity—affects every piece of tonal music. In the broadest sense, then, when we speak of the rhythm of a given piece, we are referring to the durational patterns of all its lines separately and combined; to the durational patterns of its harmonic changes and of its textural, timbral, dynamic, and articulation changes; to all the factors that give rise to accentuations of varying strengths on a variety of levels; to its motivic, phrasing, and formal subdivisions; and to its continuity and flow. That any comprehensive discussion of musical rhythm is also in some sense a discussion of style is inevitable, since these are the factors that in union add up to style.

A comprehensive discussion of all of these factors in the entire historic sweep of tonal music is of course beyond the scope of any single study. This book concentrates on a number of areas that have generated considerable controversy in recent studies of rhythm: the nature of accent and meter, levels of meter, and the interaction of various aspects of rhythm. Its aim is twofold: to illuminate the issues and implications that bear on various positions in these controversies and to promote appreciation of the full range of rhythms in tonal music.

2
ACCENT

The term accent is of such currency among musicians that it comes as a surprise to a scholar to realize how divergent and inadequate most of its definitions are. All musicians "know" what accent means; it is a central concern of most theorists who have written about rhythm. Yet many studies of rhythm in the past did not even attempt a definition of the term. Those definitions that have been proposed either limit themselves to only a single aspect of accent or confuse various aspects. Several factors are responsible for these inadequate definitions:

1. *The failure to differentiate between accent as an aspect of performance and accent as an inherent quality of a note or event.* Robert Donington, in the articles on accent and accentuation in *The New Grove,* considers only the performance aspect.

Accent. The prominence given by a more or less sudden and conspicuous increase in volume, or by a slight lengthening of the duration, or by a minute preceding silence of articulation, or by any combination of these means.

Certainly, a performer might use these mannerisms to project an accent on any note. But an accented note or event remains accented even if no performance mannerism emphasizes it. Most obvious is a note or event occurring on a metric accent—the downbeat of a measure, for instance, is accented whether or not it is played "with an accent."

2. *The failure to differentiate between dynamic intensification (stress) and other types of accent.* Dynamic intensification is one kind of accent. But notes or events need not be loud to be accented. There are other types of accent, most obviously metric accents, that

occur whether or not the accented note receives a dynamic intensification. Indeed, a performance that made a noticeable stress on each downbeat would, for many pieces, be a thumping bore.

Cooper and Meyer propose a distinction between the concepts of *stress* ("dynamic intensification") and *accent* ("a stimulus which is *marked for consciousness* in some way").[1] Their dramatic illustration of the difference between the two is the downbeat of measure 280 from the first movement of the *"Eroica" Symphony*—a silent downbeat on which the preceding tutti leads us to expect a climactic harmonic resolution. "The first beat of measure 280 must be the loudest silence in musical literature" (p. 139). I adopt the distinction between accent and stress proposed by Cooper and Meyer, with the difference that I consider stress a type of accent, not a different category of emphasis.

3. *The failure to differentiate between poetic accent and musical accent.* The first of the recent studies of rhythm, that by Cooper and Meyer (1960), borrows from poetic scansion the symbols — and ‿ for strong and weak.[2] Cone, too, adopts these symbols, sometimes differentiating two types of strong accents: / for an initiating accent of a phrase, and \ for a concluding accent.[3] In the works of both authors, these symbols are applied to passages on several levels, as in example 2-1.

2–1. Schubert, *Symphony No. 5,* third movement, as analyzed by Cooper and Meyer (example 117)

But there are crucial differences between poetic and musical accent.[4] Poetic scansion knows only the difference between accented and unaccented; in music there is a range of accentual strengths. Poetic scansion considers an accented syllable strong until the arrival of the following unaccented syllable. In music, only the attack of an accented note, beat, or event can be considered strong because subdivisions of that note, beat, or event may be weaker than either the attack of the accented note, beat, or event or

14

the attack of a following unaccented note, beat, or event. Musical accentuation is thus a multitiered phenomenon. Consider the nature of metric accents in example 2-2. The first attack may be the strongest of the measure, but all the beat subdivisions between the first and second half notes are weaker than the attack of either note. That is, if the first half note is divided into two quarters, into four eighths, eight sixteenths, or any other subdivisions, all subdivisions beginning after the downbeat are weaker than the attack of either beat 1 or beat 3.

$$\frac{4}{4} \quad \textbf{\textit{d}} \quad \textbf{\textit{d}} \quad \| $$

2–2

The difference between poetic and musical accent is the difference between considering accent a property of a span of time or a property of a point in time. Whereas poetic accent refers to a span of time, musical accent is the property of a point in time.

The discussion of example 2-2 has already demonstrated one way in which the treatment of musical accent as a span of time contradicts our everyday understanding of musical structure. When the concept of accent as a span of time is applied to large-scale accentual patterns, as in the works of Cooper and Meyer or those of Cone, these problems increase. Cooper and Meyer, for instance, assert that measures 5–8 of example 2-1 are accented in relation to measures 1–4 (see level 4 of their analysis). But neither Cooper and Meyer nor Cone, in similar analyses, specify how or where these measures are strong. Are we to understand the entire four measures, including every note, as strong? Only by considering accents as points in time can we avoid such problems.

4. *The failure to differentiate metric accents from other types of accent.* Most studies on rhythm, either explicitly or implicitly, consider accentuation solely in terms of metric accent. Komar, for instance, treats accent implicitly only in terms of the metric hierarchy. Cooper and Meyer, in their definitional discussion of accent, refer briefly to accents of *notes* or *tones* (p. 7) but then abruptly shift to discussing accent and unaccent only as properties of *beats* (p. 8). Berry, too, discusses accent principally in terms of meter. "*Accent* is a theoretical term denoting the relative projective, qualitative strength of a given impulse as compared with others which precede and follow it and, with it, form a metric unit at a given level."[5]

Linking the concept of accent to that of beat or pulse leads some writers to deny that various types of accent, among them dynamic stresses and syncopations, are accents at all. Cooper and Meyer, as noted earlier, define dynamic stress not as a type of accent but as a different category of emphasis altogether. They also avoid calling syncopations accents.[6] Berry, Komar, and Arnold Schoenberg relocate the barlines in some examples so that obviously accented notes fall on the new downbeats.[7] Such redefinitions contradict common parlance among musicians, who use the term accent to refer to types of emphasis other than metric accents.

Of greater importance to a study of rhythm, the linking of accent and beat precludes investigation into the factors that cause accents and into the factors that give rise to beats and meter. Among recent studies of rhythm, John Graziano's dissertation on accent is unique in studying separately the factors that cause accent in order to understand the relationship between accent and meter.[8] This chapter and chapter 3 also pursue such an investigation.

A Definition of Accent

An accent is a point of emphasis. In order for a point in musical time to be accented, something must occur to mark that point. It is the beginning of a musical event that marks off accented points in time. Accents are, therefore, *points of initiation*. The beginning of a note, for example, is accented both in relation to the preceding silence or the sustained portion of the preceding note and in relation to the sustained portion of that note. The beginning of a new dynamic level, especially a loud one, is accented in relation to the preceding dynamic level and to the continuation of the new dynamic level. The beginning of a pattern or motive is accented in relation to the interior of the preceding pattern and to the continuation of that pattern. The beginning of a harmony is accented in relation to the continuation of the preceding harmony and the continuation of the new harmony, and so forth.[9]

Metric accents seem to be an exception to this rule. A metric accent, after all, can occur on a rest; no event need mark it off. This is because meter is, in part, a psychological phenomenon. When a meter is first established, or is being reinforced, events must mark off or imply the metrically strong points. Once established, however, a meter has a life of its own. This issue will be discussed in detail later in this chapter and in chapter 3. In any event, metric accents are points of initiation like other accents: downbeats begin measures, interior beats in a measure mark off the beginnings of measure subdivisions, and beat subdivisions mark off the beginnings of parts of beats.

With a definition of accent as an emphasis on a point of initiation, the focus of study turns to the factors that set accents apart from the surrounding points in musical time. Before we begin this study, two caveats are in order. Cooper and Meyer as well as other writers on rhythm have warned of the dangers of treating individual rhythmic factors in isolation. Outside of the hothouse of hypothetical examples, single factors rarely if ever operate without other factors being present. The effect we attribute to one cause may equally be the product of other factors. This section treats the factors that give rise to accents in tonal music. Any given accent in an example may arise from any of several factors working separately or together. If only one factor is mentioned in the accompanying discussion, it is because that is the factor under consideration and because that factor does play a role in creating the accent. Later sections of this chapter and chapter 3 explore the conjunction of several factors.

Second, accent is a relative, not an absolute quality. A note or event is accented in relation to another note or event. In example 2-3, for instance, the beginning of every sixteenth is metrically accented in relation to any subdivisions of that sixteenth. The second and fourth sixteenths of each beat are metrically unaccented in relation to the first and third sixteenths. The third sixteenth of each beat is metrically accented in relation to the second and fourth and metrically unaccented in relation to the first, and so forth.

2–3

FACTORS THAT GIVE RISE TO ACCENT

Long Durations

Longer durations following shorter durations are accented. In example 2-4, for instance, the half notes are accented. We will refer to such accents as *durational accents*—specifically, accents caused by a relatively long duration following one or more shorter durations. (Some writers use the term *agogic accent* for the accent caused by relatively long notes. But since agogic has other meanings in performance, durational accent is used in this book.) It is the length of a long note that causes the note to receive a durational accent. Although this may appear tautological, it does illuminate the reason that longer notes are accented. Following shorter notes, the single attack of a long note initiates a longer span uninterrupted by lower-level attacks or accents. As a result, the durationally accented note initiates a more long-range context than the shorter notes that precede it.[10]

> indicates durational accents.

2–4

Durational accents are powerful in any context. They often help us locate basic metric units, as at the opening of the pieces in example 2-5. And when durational accents do not agree with the meter, the result is a form of syncopation, as in the works in example 2-6.

Mozart, *Piano Sonata*, K. 545, first movement

Brahms, *Violin Concerto*, op. 77, first movement

2–5

Accent

Bach, *Violin Concerto in A Minor,* first movement

Beethoven, *Piano Sonata,* op. 13, third movement

> indicates durational accents

2–5. (Continued)

Schumann, *Faschingsschwank aus Wien,* op. 26, first movement

Brahms, *Symphony No. 4,* op. 98, fourth movement

2–6

Consecutive Durational Accents. Durational accents are perceived in relation to preceding durations. In example 2-7, for instance, each of the last three durations receives a durational accent. As we hear the rhythm, we hear only one duration at a time. During the eighth note, we hear its length relative to the preceding sixteenth. But we have not yet perceived the length of any following durations. Similarly, the quarter note receives a durational accent in relation to the preceding eighth, and the half note receives a durational accent in relation to the quarter.

2–7

Because of the accumulation of accents, rhythmic patterns with successive durational accents provide quite emphatic accentuations on the final duration, especially if the final duration is longer than the total of any preceding activity. This is true of many rhythms of the first movement of Beethoven's *Seventh Symphony* (example 2-8). Imagine how much weaker the profile of the passage would be if it were without the consecutive durational accents, as in example 2-9.

Vivace (♩. = 104)

2–8. Beethoven, *Symphony No. 7*, op. 92, first movement

2–9

Durational Accents of Other Factors. Durational accents arise not only in single parts but in any musical aspect that defines patterns of durations. In the closing measures of the first movement of Beethoven's *Fifth Symphony*, op. 67, the entire texture participates in the durational accents of measures 492, 494, 496, and 500.

Changes in the harmonic rhythm can give rise to durational accents. This is especially common at the ends of phrases, where an acceleration in the rate of harmonic change often precedes a relatively long final harmony. The durational accent in the harmonic rhythm then supports the arrival of the cadential goal. Review measures 3 and 6 in example 1-4. See also the Mozart phrase in example 1-5. The change from a new harmony every three beats in measures 1–7 to a new harmony every two beats in measures 8 and 9 with one-beat harmonic inflections at the end of measure 9 leads to the durational accent in the harmonic rhythm on the downbeat of measure 10. A similar speed-up and durational accent on measure 10 occurs in the melodic rhythm. If the acceleration in harmonic rhythm were not present, as in example 2-10, the arrival on the final harmony would be rather lame.

2–10

New Events

The point at which any new event begins is accented. As we have already noted, this is trivially true of the beginning of any note. The following are some other manifestations.

Pitch Change. In a melody or other part with no repeated pitches, the rhythm of pitch change is the durational pattern of the part. The rhythm of pitch change is of greater interest in a part featuring repeated pitches. At the very beginning of Beethoven's *Fifth Symphony*, for instance, the pitch changes reinforce the durational accents (example 2-11). We may often think of this motive as primarily durational, overlooking the role that pitch change plays in creating that rhythm. Imagine how much weaker the rhythmic profile of this motive (example 2-12) would be if the accents caused by pitch change did not agree with the durational accents.

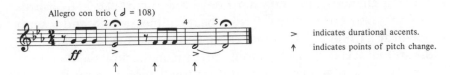

2–11. Beethoven, *Symphony No. 5*, op. 67, first movement

> indicates durational accents.
↑ indicates points of pitch change.

2–12

The ensuing measures of the *Fifth Symphony* (example 2-13) demonstrate a number of interactions between pitch changes and other types of accents. Immediately following the second fermata, every second melodic pitch change coincides either with a durational accent or with a downbeat of a measure. The remaining pitch changes occur on the second eighth of each measure. It is the presence of these pitch changes on a metrically weak subdivision that adds so much dynamism to the rhythm of this passage. How much less dramatic and more singsong are the alternatives in example 2-14 that coordinate the rhythm of pitch changes with the meter.

When the pattern of pitch change departs from the three repeated eighths (beginning in measure 14), durational accents continue to appear on downbeats, while the repeated eighths that remain still begin on the second eighth of the measure. Thus, the

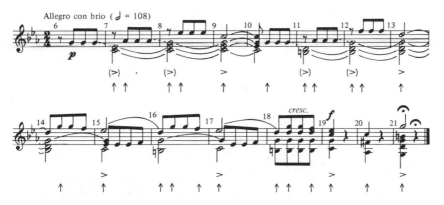

> indicates durational accents in the melody.

↑ indicates points of pitch change in the melody.

2–13. Beethoven, *Symphony No. 5,* op. 67, first movement

2–14

downbeats are still reinforced and the second eighth of many measures retains its impetus. After another pair of fermatas, the opening motive recurs in its initial rhythmic profile. Then new derivations appear in which pitch changes and durational accents again provide the rhythmic dynamism (example 2-15).

Noncoordination of pitch changes and durational accents helps create the melodic rhythm in the opening melody of Mozart's *Symphony No. 40* (example 2-16). Imagine how much more accented the quarter notes would be, and how much more stilted the phrase as a whole would become, if the pitch changes were coordinated with the quarter notes (example 2-17). The noncoordination

23

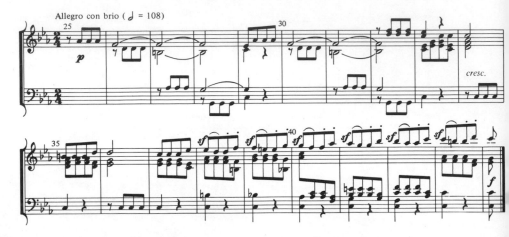

2–15. Beethoven, *Symphony No. 5,* op. 67, first movement

> indicates durational accents.
↑ indicates points of pitch change.

2–16. Mozart, *Symphony No. 40,* K. 550, first movement

> indicates durational accents.
↑ indicates points of pitch change.

2–17

of pitch changes with the beat in passages featuring rapid notes is often a principal factor in creating the rhythmic dynamism of a passage, as in example 2-18. In other passages, the coordination of pitch changes with metric accents supports the meter, creating quite a different effect (example 2-19).

24

Bach, *Brandenburg Concerto No. 4,* first movement

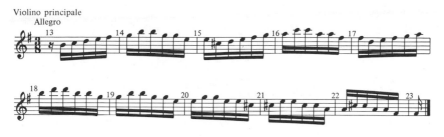

Schumann, *String Quartet,* op. 41, no. 3, second movement

2–18

Bach, *Brandenburg Concerto No. 5,* first movement

Schumann, *Symphony No. 4,* op. 120, third movement

2–19

Harmonic Change. The groups of notes that we call harmonies in tonal music are of critical importance to musical meaning. A harmony defines the status of every pitch occurring during its span as a stable member of that harmony, as a more mobile member of that harmony (such as a chord seventh), or as a relatively transient nonharmonic tone. The harmony stands in a linear and a functional relationship both to preceding and following harmonies and to the prevailing tonic. The change from one harmony to another is a change from one constellation of pitch relationships to another. The point at which this change occurs is always a point of accent in relation to the sustained portion of that harmony and of any preceding harmony.

Harmonic change is a powerful source of accent. There is no need here to demonstrate that harmonic change in tonal music generally occurs at metrically strong points on some level. Indeed, chapter 3 demonstrates that harmonic change is a primary factor in establishing meter. With the sole exception of the upbeat to a phrase, harmonic changes do not often begin on a weak beat or beat subdivision and continue through the following stronger division. Perusal of any of the examples introduced thus far or of most tonal excerpts will bear this out.

When harmonic changes do occur before strong beat divisions, as in measure 8 of example 2-20, other factors often clarify the situation. In the Beethoven passage, durational accents in the

Beethoven, *Piano Sonata*, op. 31, no. 1, first movement

Brahms, *Symphony No. 3*, op. 90, first movement

2–20

composite rhythm show that the sixteenth upbeats to measures 1 and 4–9 in the right hand are anticipations of the chords. The effect is not a distortion of the placement of harmonic changes but perhaps a parody of a performance mannerism (playing with uncoordinated hands). In the Brahms passage, the changes are more disruptive to the sense of continued meter.

When harmonic changes occur on weak beats or weak beat di-

27

visions and there are no factors supporting the notated beats, the continuation of the meter may itself be in question. See example 2-21. Only if the listener maintains the previous meter will these passages be heard in the notated meter.

2–21. Beethoven, *Piano Sonata*, op. 101, first movement

Textural Change. Textural changes, especially when they are sudden, are a source of accent. These accents affect both large-scale and local contexts. Listen to the passage in example 2-22. The change to tutti in measure 16 creates a textural change accent, supported by accented changes in dynamics, register, and duration. Within the tutti, textural changes of lesser scope, such as the reduction to octaves in the moving parts on the second beat of measures 17 and 19–23, give rise to accents. In measures 20–24, the entrance of the full chords on each downbeat provides accents confirming the notated meter (supported by harmonic and registral changes).

At the measure level, textural accents commonly operate to support the meter, to promote rhythmic continuity, or to do both. In measures 19–24 of example 2–22, for instance, the combinations of accents—harmonic and textural changes on the downbeats, textural changes on the second beats, and durational accents

2–22. Haydn, *Symphony No. 104*, first movement

on the third beats—enliven these measures much like the combinations of accents discussed at the opening of Beethoven's *Fifth*. The accents in measures 16–24 of this Haydn symphony demonstrate that textural change accents can be caused by changes to both a denser or thinner texture, and to both a larger or smaller registral scope. What is important in creating a sense of accent is that the change be sudden *at the level under consideration*. The entrance of the tutti in measure 16, for instance, following a long passage in another texture, acts in a large-scale context. The remaining textural change accents discussed in measures 17–24 act on a more local level.

Textural Accents

One type of textural accent is caused by attacks in many or all voices of a texture. These points of density are accented in relation to those points at which only one or a few voices have attacks. The range of possibilities is enormous, from the totally unified attacks that open Mozart's *Eine Kleine Nachtmusik*, K. 525, or Tchaikovsky's *Romeo and Juliet,* or that conclude many a composition, to the single attacks that open Schumann's *Dichterliebe* (see example 2-24) or Brahms' *Intermezzo*, op. 119, no. 1. In most pieces, there is a range of textural interactions, with some relatively accented in relation to others. At the opening of Mozart's *Symphony No. 40,* for instance, there are three textural components: the continuous eighth-note accompaniment, the bass notes, and the

29

melody. Attacks in all three components coincide only on down-beats beginning in measure 2—a factor that reinforces the notated meter (example 2-23).

2–23. Mozart, *Symphony No. 40*, K. 550, first movement

At the opening of *Im wunderschönen Monat Mai* from Schumann's *Dichterliebe* (example 2-24), the individual attacks of the opening measures lead to the unified attacks of all voices at the end of measure 5 as the harmonically hesitant and unresolved opening moves to a cadence in A major. The cadential strength evaporates with the return to individual attacks in measure 6.[11]

As with other types of accentuation, context is all-important. Nearly every beat in the opening phrase of example 2-23 is more accented (because of simultaneous attacks between melody and inner voices) than most of example 2-24. In terms of the projection of relatively accented points within each excerpt, it is the relative accentuation in that context that matters.

The Entrance of a Voice. Another type of textural accent occurs at the point at which a voice enters. This type of accent can assist in the cumulative activity of the stretto of a fugue, as well as in the pseudo-imitative texture Beethoven uses in many passages of the *Fifth Symphony*, first movement. Review examples 2-13 and 2-15.

Even in nonimitative passages, or in passages that are not truly contrapuntal, the accents caused by the entrance of new components of the texture can be quite important to the overall rhythm. In measures 280–84 from Tchaikovsky's *Romeo and Juliet* (example 2-25), the separate entrances of all components of the texture other

2-24. Schumann, *Dichterliebe,* op. 48, no. 1

than the horn melody occur on weak beats or weak metric subdivisions.

Later in the same piece, increasingly complex accent patterns caused by the separate entrances of textural components (measures 320ff.) lead to the reduction to only two textural components after measure 334 and eventually to the unified texture of the recapitulation at measure 352. The transition from diversified textural accents toward the unified accentuations of the recapitulation complements the harmonic motion toward the recapitulation.

New Registers. Another type of textural accent occurs on the appearance of a new register, either in a single part or in an entire texture. Review Haydn's *Symphony No. 104* in example 2-22 for a passage in which other accents are coordinated with a sudden expansion of both the higher and lower registers. Such new registers need not be far removed from the preceding register in an absolute sense to produce accents. In the opening phrase subdivision of Mozart's *Symphony No. 40,* for instance, the melodic B♭ is a dramatic

2–25. Tchaikovsky, *Romeo and Juliet*

addition to a melody that has remained within a semitone prior to that point. (Review example 2-16.) Placing the B♭ apart from the durational accent on the downbeat maintains the supple rhythm of this melody. (Review the discussion of the rhythm of pitch change and durational accents in the phrase in examples 2-16 and 2-17.) Imagine how this quality would be marred if the B♭ were to occur on the downbeat of measure 3 instead of on the second beat (example 2-26). The coincidence of the registral accent with a durational and a metric accent in example 2-26 creates a strong point of accentuation out of character with the remainder of this passage.

2–26

Contour Changes

Notes that stand at the top or bottom of a melody or melodic segment are accented. Such accents are called *contour accents*. Contour accents are points of initiation because the accented note stands at the beginning of a new melodic direction. Contour accents of high notes are generally more prominent than those of low notes. The reason for this may be that melodies are often the highest voice in a tonal texture. The lower melodic notes may be in registers close to the accompaniment. But the upper notes of the melody are often the very highest in the entire texture. In a melody such as that in example 2-27, the contour accents complement the durational

2–27. Beethoven, *Piano Sonata*, op. 2, no. 1, first movement

accents to reinforce the downbeats of measure 2 and measures 4–7. Without the contour accents on these downbeats, the melodic rhythm would be quite different (example 2-28).

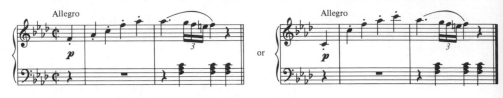

2–28

In some melodies, a contour accent is equivalent to the introduction of a new register. Review the opening of Mozart's *Symphony No. 40* in example 2-16. Listen also to the excerpt from Bach's *Sonata in C Major for Violin Alone* in example 2-29. Contour accents appear on two levels here. First is the note-to-note interaction that causes the bass and top notes to be accented in relation to the middle register. These accents are noted in example 2-29. At a larger level are the contour accents within the highest line (example 2-30).

2–29. Bach, *Sonata in C for Violin Alone,* fourth movement

2–30

Contour accents are most prominent when there are relatively few clear-cut contour changes in a melody or a part. The contour accents noted at the opening of Beethoven's *F Minor Piano Sonata*

34

in example 2-27 are particularly crucial notes in that melody. When a melody contains frequent changes of direction, such as the note-to-note continuity in the Bach melody in example 2-29, the power of any one of these contour accents is diminished because there are so many in the immediate vicinity. As we discussed earlier in this chapter, accent is a relative concept. The more criteria there are to create accent in a given context, the more active that context, but the less prominent the accent caused by any single occurrence of a criterion.

2–31. Mozart, *Piano Sonata*, K. 545, first movement, left hand only

It is in part for this reason that arpeggiation patterns such as Alberti basses become relatively neutral backgrounds for melodies. One could assert that a pattern such as that in example 2-31 represents the three illustrated voices with the vigorous rhythmic interaction implied. But in fact, the contour changes on every note neutralize each other in the accompaniment.

Dynamics

The onset of a loud dynamic is so universally recognized as a creator of accentuation that examples are not needed to demonstrate it. The loud dynamic may be the sudden beginning of a long section after a much softer dynamic, the peak of a crescendo, or merely a slightly louder attack on individual notes.

It is essential to consider the type of instrument when assessing a dynamic accent. Some instruments—among them the piano—introduce every note with a loud attack followed by a diminuendo. Yet listeners who are familiar with the articulative range of the piano hear legato passages in which there seem to be no sharp attacks.

Were a violin or flute to play a legato passage with the dynamics produced by a piano, the result would be anything but legato. As with so many other aspects of accent, it is the relative strength of the accent in relation to other accents in that context that will determine the presence of a dynamic accent.

Articulation

In all passages that group notes under articulation slurs, accents arise at the beginning of each slur. Although all performers are aware of this, string and wind players are perhaps most conscious of the accentual effects of articulation because of the necessity of choosing bowings, tonguings, and places for breathing.

The various articulations of a familiar étude in example 2-32 readily demonstrate the effect of articulation on accentuation.

etc.

2–32. Kreutzer, *Etude No. 2 for Violin,* bowings added

Articulation accents often complement other accents in a melody, such as durational accents, accents caused by harmonic change, and contour accents (example 2-33).

2–33. Mendelssohn, *Violin Concerto,* op. 64, first movement, violin solo

2–33. *(Continued)*

But articulation accents can also add new accentuation patterns not directly implied by "the notes themselves" (example 2-34).

Mendelssohn, *Violin Concerto*, op. 64, first movement violin solo

Tchaikowsky, *The Nutcracker, March,* violins

2–34

Pattern (Motive) Beginnings

The beginning of any motivic pattern receives an accent. Perhaps the best way to demonstrate the effect of this type of accent is to change a passage so as to alter the motives. Example 2-35 presents the opening of Mozart's *Symphony No. 40* and a revision of the melody omitting the upbeat. In Mozart's version, the melodic motive begins on the upbeat. But without the first upbeat to each phrase subdivision, the pattern repetitions (the motives) begin on the strong beats. The coordination of the pattern-beginning accents with durational, harmonic-change, and textural accents in the revision robs Mozart's melody of some of its suppleness. (Compare the similar effect of the pitch-change rhythm already noted in examples 2-16 and 2-17.)

37

> indicates pattern-beginning accent.

⌞___⌟ indicates melodic motive.

2–35. Mozart, *Symphony No. 40*, K. 550, first movement, violin

Other Factors Not Considered Here

Some theorists have proposed additional factors as creators of accents. Among these studies, John Graziano's dissertation is unique in that it discusses various factors that contribute to accent. Graziano's inquiry concerns "accent as it occurs at the metric level [i.e., the measure level] in relation to the phrase."[12] Graziano discusses some of the factors treated earlier in this chapter, among them durational accents in single lines and textures, textural accents, dynamic accents, pitch-change accents, and accents caused by new registers (although he uses different terms for many of these). Some other factors that he includes do not play a role in the present study. Among these are the accentual properties of melodic intervals. Graziano asserts that some intervals are end-accented (ascending minor seconds and perfect fourths, and descending major seconds, major thirds, and perfect fifths), some intervals are beginning-accented (ascending major seconds, major thirds, and perfect fifths and descending minor seconds, minor thirds, and perfect fourths), and the remaining intervals are neutral in terms of accentuation.[13] These conclusions are based on the research of a number of psychologists, most of whom played isolated pairs of intervals and asked subjects to decide which note seemed accented or final.

Whatever the value of such interpretations concerning isolated pitch-pairs (and Graziano is aware of the importance of context in assessing the strength of such accents), in the context of a musical passage, these alleged accentuations do not seem to create perceptible accents. Consider the opening of Haydn's "Quinten"

38

Quartet in example 2-36. Each of the indicated pitches is either the accented first or second note of a pitch-pair according to Graziano's hypothesis. The resulting accentuation does not seem to be a property of this melody.

> indicates supposed intervallic accents
according to Graziano's criteria.

2–36. Haydn, *String Quartet,* op. 76, no. 2, first movement

A second factor cited by Graziano as causing accent, but one that is rejected here, is the accented value of harmonic functions. Graziano regards an arrival on the tonic, for instance, as the recipient of an accent.[14] There is a long tradition of attempting to equate various kinds of harmonic functions in terms of their inherent accentual qualities. William Caplin, in a recent article, summarizes the theories of the major contributors to this tradition (Rameau, Vogler, Sechter, Hauptmann, and Riemann), concluding that there has been little agreement among theorists and little agreement between the assertions of these theorists and compositional practice.[15]

In rejecting the notion that some harmonic functions are inherently accented, Berry argues that "tonal function . . . is in and of itself *metrically neutral:*

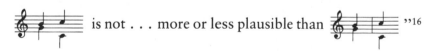

To be sure, some tonal harmonies almost always occur in a particular metric position. The cadential $^6_4$, for instance, virtually always arrives on a beat as strong as or stronger than the beat on which the ensuing dominant arrives. But if one regards the cadential $^6_4$ as an attack chord on the arrival of a dominant, as theorists as diverse as Rameau, Riemann, and Schenker have done, then the accentual position of the cadential $^6_4$ is the result of avoiding syncopation in the harmonic rhythm, not the result of some inherent accentual quality of the chord.

The dissonant portion of a suspension has also been cited as the location of an accent.[17] Once again, it is the fact of harmonic change that causes the accent. After all, a suspension can only become dissonant when a harmonic change occurs.

Carl Schachter, drawing on an idea by Victor Zuckerkandl, argues for accentual properties of scale degrees in the major scale.[18] Most listeners, when hearing an ascending or descending major scale played slowly, will, as Schachter and Zuckerkandl assert, hear the notes below scale step 5 tend downward toward an accented tonic and the notes above scale step 5 tend upward toward an accented tonic. But like the accentual characteristics of isolated intervals cited by Graziano, any accentuations caused by placement of scale degrees are overwhelmed by other factors in the context of an actual piece. As a single example, review the scales in measures 8 and 9 of the Mozart phrase in example 1-5. The appearances of the tonic G in these scales do not have a discernible accentual effect on the passage.

EVALUATING THE ACCENT-PRODUCING FACTORS

The preceding section of this chapter introduces quite a few factors that give rise to accents in a musical passage. These factors may act in concert to produce relatively strong accents at a few locations, or they may act separately to produce a string of weaker accents. Discussion of several of the musical examples has noted the coordination or noncoordination of various types of accent in a given passage.

We might proceed at this point to line up all the accent-producing factors in a passage and see where various accents are coordinated. We might then conclude that the greater the number of accent-producing factors that converge on a given note or event, the greater the strength of the accent on that note or event. But such an approach would ignore three considerations. First, not all accent-producing factors operate with equal importance. Some factors by themselves can produce a more powerful accent than several other factors combined. Second, accents in a musical passage occur in a metric context. The meter is both the product of certain patterns of accentuation, and also, once established, a strong influence on accentuation. Third, our ability to perceive different kinds of accents in a passage depends in part on how well we know that passage—that is, on how well we are able to appreciate certain types of accentuation as they occur instead of after they have passed. Each consideration merits comment.

Differences among the Factors That Produce Accents

Accents that are produced by factors involving only pitch or duration are more deeply embedded in a musical structure than accents produced by other factors. Harmonic-change accents, pitch-change accents, durational accents, pattern-beginning accents, and so forth, are of a different nature than dynamic stresses, articulation accents, texture accents, and so forth. This is due to the primacy that pitch and duration have in our conception of music. Whatever that elusive object of our perceptions may be that we call a musical composition, specific pitch relationships in specific durational relationships are a principal factor in defining a piece and differentiating one piece from another. Two different pieces may be alike in timbre (orchestration), texture, tempo, articulations, and dynamics. But if they differ in pitches and durations, we will not consider them the same piece. Yet we immediately recognize different versions of the same piece—for instance, a piano transcription of an orchestral work—even though the versions may differ significantly in timbre, texture (in the sense that accompaniment patterns may be changed, doublings added or removed, and so forth), articulation (in the sense that the piano is incapable of the true legato of many orchestral instruments), and dynamics (in the sense that the dynamic range of a piano is different from that of an orchestra, and a piano makes a diminuendo on every note).

Similarly, our attitude toward a performer's interpretation of a piece reflects the primacy of pitch and rhythm. We are usually willing to grant a performer considerable latitude in interpreting the tempo, the dynamics, and the articulations (bowings, for instance). To the extent that these aspects differ from those notated in the score, we acknowledge the performer's interpretation. But let a performance depart from the score in pitches or in durations (to the extent that one duration can be misheard as another), and we will complain of a wrong note or a wrong rhythm. (Exceptions are, of course, those passages for which convention admits improvisation.) As a result, those accentuations that are inherent in the pitches and durations of a piece will be projected in any "correct" performance. But accentuations caused by other factors will vary, sometimes greatly, from one performance to another.

Accents in the Context of Meter

Virtually all tonal passages feature a regular meter. The metric hierarchy of relatively accented and relatively unaccented points in time colors all other types of accentuation. The regularity of accentuation in the metric hierarchy, often over long stretches of time, creates expectations according to which we expect certain points in time to be accented—hence, we may attribute accentuations to factors occurring at the metrically accented points in time even when those factors would not necessarily give rise to marked accent in the absence of that meter.

One of the advantages of separating the concept of accent from that of beat is the resulting ability to study the accentual factors that give rise to beats. For different accentual factors may create a meter in different contexts (as discussed in chapter 3). A major difference between metric accents and the other types of accentuations discussed in this chapter is that a given metric accent may occur at a point where no accent-producing factor is present. (Remember the "loud silence" in measure 280 of the "Eroica's" first movement.) Whereas other types of accent require some factor to mark off the accented point in time, the metric hierarchy has a life of its own. Once that structure is established, we as performers or listeners will keep it going as long as it is not strongly contradicted by other evidence. Accentual features that may not be powerful enough to establish a meter may be the only accentuations to occur on metrically strong points after the meter is under way.[19]

Immediately Perceptible Factors Versus Those Requiring Familiarity with the Piece

As we listen to a piece of music, we perceive the piece as it unfolds in time. When we hear a piece for the first time, we can know the notes and events we have already heard (to the extent that we can remember them) and the note and event we are currently hearing. But we cannot know the notes or events that are yet to come. In the case of a single note, for instance, we cannot, at its beginning, know how long it is to last. In the case of a dynamic, we cannot know if a note louder than the previous note is only one stage in a crescendo or whether it is the peak of the crescendo. In the case of a melody line, we cannot know if a given note is the high point of the phrase or merely one step on the way to that high point. As a result, it is difficult to imagine how we might perceive the accents created by these factors. We perceive an accent as an impulse at the point at which a note or event begins. Even if we retroactively recognize that a note is, say, durationally accented, that it is the peak of a crescendo, or that it is the high point in a melody, we cannot return to the point in time at which that note began and attribute its accent to it. Such *ex post facto* elements affect our perception of the accent only on later hearings of that passage—whether in repetitions or transformations within the piece or on later hearings of the entire piece.

But certain factors that cause accents are perceptible at the initiation of a note or an event. The beginning of a note, the entrance of a new harmony, the beginning of a new texture, the beginning of a new timbre, the opening of a new register—factors such as these are immediately perceptible even on the very first hearing of an unfamiliar piece.

As we get to know a piece, even during that first hearing, the differences between these categories of accent-causing factors diminish. When a melody or a motive recurs, we begin to recognize and remember various features. We begin to expect that certain notes will indeed be long even if we cannot know that for sure on their initiation. We can assume that the high point of a melody or the peak of a crescendo will occur at a specific point. We can assume that motives will recur in certain circumstances. And as we hear a piece repeatedly, as we begin to recall many of its features as they occur, as we begin to anticipate many features, and as we begin to memorize even more subtle features of the piece, the distinction between these categories of accent-producing factors may fade entirely.

Although this distinction between accent-causing factors may be minimal in pieces we know well, it continues to function in pieces new or relatively new to a given listener. That some of the rhythmic and metric structure of an unfamiliar piece is clear to us even on first hearing indicates that the immediately perceptible factors alone can give rise to certain essential rhythmic and metric perceptions. And that we continue to discover subtle rhythmic and metric features in familiar pieces indicates that the factors requiring memory and anticipation also affect the rhythmic structure.

Indeed, as we get to know a piece better and better, we are more and more attuned to all the nuances in the rhythmic structure of that piece. Through repeated hearings, we gradually get to know those factors that we can recognize only if we know what is to happen next. We gradually cease being affected only by the obvious factors, but are receptive to evermore subtle aspects—for example, a special turn of phrase, a unique textural accent, or a particular interaction of registral accents with pattern-change accents and with harmonic-change accents, all along with the accentuations in the metric hierarchy. We feel as if we can move to the gestures of each phrase. It is not that we have forgotten the more obvious features—it is rather that we have learned them so well that we can now follow the nuances within them.

It is in part this aspect of music that allows us—even demands of us—that we return to a beloved piece over and over again. We may read a favorite novel a few times in a lifetime. We may attend performances of a favorite play a few times. Some among us have even seen their favorite movies a dozen or more times. But we musicians and music lovers can and do return to a favorite piece many dozens of times. A performer may practice dozens or even hundreds of times a phrase that he or she knows technically until he or she is satisfied that all the gestures residing in it are fully digested.

As I noted at the beginning of chapter 1, music occurs in time. When a composition has captivated us, we relish those repeated auditions so that we can get to know better all the nuances of its time structuring, otherwise known as its rhythms.

Finally, there is the performer, who projects and interprets all the patterns of accentuation. Although all the factors, including meter, that give rise to patterns of accentuation are "in the music," it is the performer who decides how to "bring them out." This can be done by applying or not applying subtle (or not-so-subtle!) dynamic accents, by emphasizing or not emphasizing differentiations in dynamics, in articulation, in timbre, in texture, or in register, by adding subtle details of pacing, and by emphasizing or underplaying various other features (such as making clear harmonic changes as opposed to blurring points of harmonic change, or emphasizing a unified attack in all parts as opposed to arpeggiating slightly a unison attack). By these and other means, a performer can emphasize or underplay many accent-producing factors.

As a result, a full picture of accent cannot be gained solely by studying the individual features that give rise to accent. The interaction of all these features both creates and is affected by the larger context. This chapter has discussed the various factors that give rise to accent. Chapter 3 begins the discussion of context with a study of the establishment, the nature, and the effects of meter.

3

METER

Most musicians agree that meter refers to the organization of beats or pulses into patterns containing an accented (or strong) beat followed by one or more unaccented (or weak) beats. Two separate components are thus necessary for the existence of a meter: a stream of beats or pulses, and an organization of those beats or pulses into accented and unaccented ones.

Beyond this, there is little consensus concerning the nature of meter. Some musicians discuss meter as a phenomenon on a single level. Others argue that meter operates on many levels—that the strong beats at one level are the pulses organized by the next level. Musicians also disagree on whether metric organization must be regular (that is, whether metric groups must maintain the same patterning of strong and weak beats) or whether metric groups may change in the course of a passage.

The first section of this chapter defines the basic terms concerning meter that are used in this study. Preference, as elsewhere here, is for broad definitions that can be modified by adjectives to fit individual circumstances rather than narrow definitions that can limit the scope of inquiry.

BASIC TERMS

Beat. Beat is often defined as that which divides time into spans of equal duration. Although this is accurate enough for some musical situations, it is inadequate to describe such common occurrences as a ritardando, an accelerando, or even a rubato. Consider, for instance, example 3-1. As the speed of the quarter notes slows down in measures 2 and 3, we hear the beat slowing down. To put it an-

3–1

other way, as the quarter notes get longer in measures 2 and 3, we hear the beats getting longer. What we certainly do not hear is anything resembling the metric structure of example 3-2.

3–2

To avoid such absurdities, a definition of the term beat must account for the possibility of its varied length. *Beats mark off functionally equivalent spans of time.* Lest this seem overly abstract, remember that in our notational system, rhythmic values (eighth notes, quarter notes, and so forth) already denote functionally equivalent spans of time in a given passage. The quarter notes in example 3-1 are an adequate notation even though in measures 2 and 3 each successive quarter stands for a longer span of time. The ritardando signifies that the pace of notes previously of equivalent length slows down. Retaining the constant quarter notes indicates the functional equivalence of the durations as they get longer. The definition of beat proposed here accounts for situations such as that in example 3-1 as well as the rubatos that affect nearly all performances.

Grouping of Beats. Theoretically, there may be any whole number of beats in a metric group (that is, a strong beat may be followed by any number of weak beats). In tonal music, however, recurring groupings of two or three beats are so common in relation to any exceptions that for all practical purposes we may consider recurring duple and triple groupings as the only ones. Larger groupings of beats indicated by a meter signature ($\frac{4}{4}$, $\frac{6}{4}$, $\frac{6}{8}$, $\frac{9}{8}$, $\frac{12}{8}$, and so forth) form compound meters—multiples of a duple or triple division.[1]

46

Levels of Metric Interaction. Two levels of activity are necessary to have a meter: the level of beats and the level at which the beats are organized. Meter is the interaction of these two levels (example 3-3).

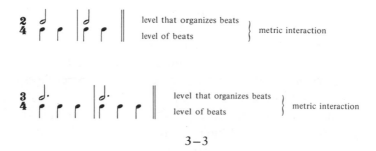

3–3

In meter signatures with 2 or 3 as their upper number, the signature denotes only a single level of metric interaction. In meter signatures with a higher number, the meter signature indicates two or more separate levels of metric organization (example 3-4).

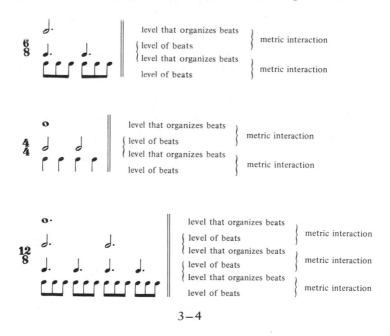

3–4

The Metric Hierarchy. Even where multiple levels of meter are not indicated by the signature, most musicians understand them to operate below the level shown in the meter signature. In $\frac{2}{4}$ meter, for instance, the quarter notes may group two eighth notes or three triplet eighths, the first of which is accented. And the eighths or triplet eighths may themselves group pairs or threesomes of sixteenths, which themselves may group even shorter note values.

This gives rise to the *metric hierarchy*. Example 3-5 displays the metric hierarchy at the opening of Mozart's *Piano Sonata*, K. 545. Accent marks (>) indicate the accented points at each metric level. Thus, the first sixteenth of each pair is accented in relation to the second sixteenth, the first eighth is accented in relation to the second eighth, and so forth.

Not all levels are articulated by the piece in all measures. The level of sixteenth-eighth interaction, for instance, arises only in occasional notes in measures 1–4 and does not appear at all in measure 12. The eighth-quarter level and the quarter-half level, on the other hand, are evident from measure 1 through the first half of measure 12.

In this Mozart excerpt, the interaction at each metric level remains the same from beginning to end. Whole notes are divided into two half notes, half notes into two quarters, quarters into two eighths, and eighths into two sixteenths throughout. This is not necessarily true of all tonal music. It is quite common for subdivisions at one level to change as, for example, when eighths change to triplets.

Also characteristic of the metric hierarchy in the Mozart passage is the fact that the metric levels nest within one another: the grouping of pulses at one level becomes the pulse at the next higher level. Most metric hierarchies in tonal music exhibit such nesting. Occasional passages, though, do contain conflicting metric groupings that do not nest. Consider the opening of Brahms' *Capriccio*, op. 76, no. 5, in example 3-6. The dotted half note subdivides into two dotted quarters (in the bass) and into three quarters (in the melody) throughout the passage. Each of these subdivisions divides into eighths at the next level. Although these two metric hierarchies agree on the length of the dotted half and the eighth note, they disagree in the interaction of the two intervening levels. Simultaneous conflicts between these and more complex metric hierarchies are a feature of much of this piece. Such conflicts in the hierarchy give the listener the choice of which structuring he or she will use to organize that level.

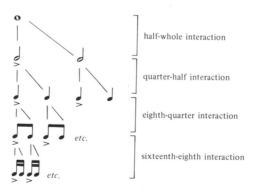

3–5. Mozart, *Piano Sonata*, K. 545, first movement

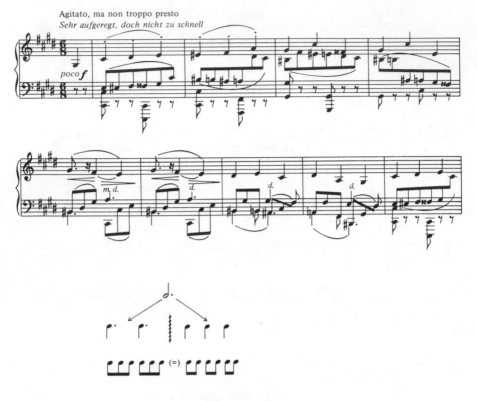

3–6. Brahms, *Capriccio,* op. 76, no. 5

The Primary Metric Level. Although there are several metric interactions in the hierarchy of most tonal passages, there is usually one level that we perceive as "the" meter of the passage. We refer to this as the *primary metric level.* The primary metric level is often the level indicated by the meter signature, although instances are common in which the meter signature reflects neither the primary metric level nor the placement of the downbeat. (See the discussion of metric notation in chapter 4.) The metric units at the primary level often reflect (indeed, are often created by) the pace of important harmonic and motivic events in the music. The beats at the primary metric level are usually one or two levels removed from the fastest note values in the passage. A fuller discussion of these points is found in the section of this chapter dealing with the factors that give rise to meter.

Regular and Irregular Meters. At the lower end of the metric hierarchy (groupings of short values), once a grouping of a specific note value has been established, the length of that grouping remains constant for the remainder of a movement in virtually all tonal music. For instance, if sixteenth notes are grouped in pairs (that is, into eighths), then it is quite exceptional for them to be grouped in threes (that is, into dotted eighths) in a subsequent passage.

Regular meter also predominates at the primary metric level in most tonal pieces. But changes in metric organization do occur. One change in the grouping of beats in triple meter is so common that it has received its own name: *hemiola*—referring to a change from 3 + 3 beats to 2 + 2 + 2 beats. See measures 8–10 of example 1-5 for instance.[2]

Hypermeter. All musicians agree that the interaction of beats and their grouping operates from the fastest note values in a piece up to the level of the notated measure. But there is considerable disagreement concerning the nature and even the existence of metric levels above that of the measure. Such levels are referred to collectively as *hypermeter.* Hypermeter covers a whole range of issues, among them those passages in which the notated measure functions as a beat, the accentual structure of phrases, regularity and irregularity at higher metric levels, the accentual structure of larger sections, the limits at which metric accents operate in long-range structures, and the nature of musical climax. Many of these issues are treated in chapters 6, 7, and 9.

Meter as a Perceptual Phenomenon. Accentuation in the metric hierarchy differs from the accentuations discussed in chapter 2 in one fundamental way. Whereas accents caused by duration, dynamics, harmonic change, texture, articulation, and the like require a particular event to create them, metric accents can exist and function without any event occurring at the moment of accent. The metric hierarchy may be established by the accentual factors in chapter 2. But it rapidly assumes a life of its own.

The listener, once he or she has recognized the pattern, internalizes the metric hierarchy. Even if a metric level is temporarily absent, that level of division or grouping remains as a latent possibility. In example 3-5, for instance, a pair of sixteenths in measure 2 divides the eighths. No further sixteenths appear until measures 4 or 5. (The notated sixteenths in measure 4 are often performed as a *Nachschlag* to the trill, not as measured sixteenths.) Yet this level of

51

activity remains as the subdivision of eights—measure 5 adds nothing new to the metric hierarchy.

The metric hierarchy, once established, functions as a grid or a structuring of time within which any event can be located at a specific position, not unlike a graph on which an object can be located on a plane surface. In this sense, meter is analogous in the rhythmic dimension of music to tonality in the realm of pitch. For just as a pitch in tonal music receives its functional meaning from its location in relation to the prevailing tonic and the prevailing harmonic-melodic interaction, an event (a note, a textural change, a dynamic change, and so forth) receives part of its rhythmic meaning from its location in the grid of measures, beats, and their subdivisions.

Knowledge of the metric position of a note or event determines part of its structural meaning. A note or event that anticipates a downbeat, or is delayed until after a downbeat, imparts quite a different effect than one that occurs on a downbeat. The predictability of a regular meter intensifies the linear and harmonic drive of tonal pitch structures. We not only expect harmonies to resolve—we expect them to resolve at specific points in time. The sense of stability or instability of a note or of a passage is strongly affected by metric position.

As a result, deciphering the metric structure of a piece is a critically important aspect of understanding and interpreting that piece. Review the Brahms *Capriccio* in example 3-6. The melodic rhythm, the location of syncopations, and even the perceived tempo depend on whether the music is heard in $\frac{6}{8}$ (in agreement with the bass) or $\frac{3}{4}$ (in agreement with the melody). Review also the passage from Beethoven's *Piano Sonata*, op. 101, in example 2-21. It goes without saying that the effect of the passage will differ radically depending on whether a listener hears the chords in measures 81–87 as syncopated or whether the listener interprets the first chord in measure 81 as a shortened downbeat (due to rubato or to a performance error) and hears the remaining chords on the beat. The same is true of much simpler contexts. A composer I know once insisted that he grew up hearing most of the first movement of Schubert's "Unfinished" *Symphony* in $\frac{6}{8}$, not in $\frac{3}{4}$ as Schubert notated it. Listen to example 3-7 and note how the music perceived in this organization differs dramatically from that found in Schubert's notation. The accentuations, the nature of syncopations, the pacing, and even the tempo are altered.

3–7

ESTABLISHING THE METRIC HIERARCHY

Out of the undifferentiated flow of time that precedes the beginning of a piece of music, the opening of that piece creates at least a part of the metric hierarchy of that piece. To establish a sense of meter, there must be at least one level of pulses and a grouping of those pulses.

Establishing a Pulse

A recurring rhythmic value or the subdivision of a longer value can establish a pulse. A recurring value that establishes a pulse is the result of the accents that begin notes. Such a recurring value may be present in either a single part in the texture or in the composite rhythm or may result from a regularity that occurs amid other durational patterns.

In the excerpts in example 3-8, one or more pulses are established by a single part. The viola part in Mozart's *Symphony No. 40* establishes the eighth-note pulse from the outset. The regularity of

Mozart, *Symphony No. 40,* first movement

Brahms, *Symphony No. 1,* op. 68, first movement

3–8

Beethoven, *Sonata for Violin and Piano,* op. 30, no. 3, first movement

3–8. *(Continued)*

the bass part also establishes a continuous pulse eight times as long. (Other factors, to be discussed later, create other pulses here.) At the opening of Brahms' *Symphony No. 1,* the steady eighth-note pedal point establishes a strong pulse underlying the complex rhythms above. The opening of Beethoven's *Violin Sonata in G* features two separate pulses in succession—first sixteenth notes, then eighth notes. The three excerpts in example 3-9 feature steady pulses that arise in the composite rhythm. At the opening of the slow movement of Mozart's "Jupiter" *Symphony* (example 3-10), quarter-note activity caused by a variety of factors (durational accents, textural accents, harmonic change accents, registral change accents, and so forth) is the only steady motion amid irregular rhythms.

Continuous activity makes palpable every unit of a pulse. But it is not necessary to hear every unit in order to know that these units exist. Many compositions open with a rhythmic value followed by a subdivision of that value. So long as the length of the subdivision is easily related to the longer value, the pulse rate represented by the shorter value is established. This occurs when the shorter value is one half, one third, or one quarter of the longer value.[3] Often, this shorter pulse rate is then confirmed as a continuous motion in the music immediately following.

In example 3-11, the single eighth in the middle of measure 1 is one third the length of the preceding and following duration. The ensuing five eighths confirm the eighth-note pulse. By the middle of measure 2 the pulse is well enough established to provide a unit of measurement for the rests in that and the following measures.

The same process occurs at differing rates in the two excerpts

Bach, *Two-Part Invention in E Major*

Haydn, *Piano Sonata*, Hob. XVI/37, third movement

Beethoven, *Symphony No. 9*, op. 125, third movement

3–9

3–10. Mozart, *Symphony No. 41*, K. 551, second movement

3–11. Mozart, *Eine Kleine Nachtmusik*, K. 525, first movement

in example 3-12. At the opening of the finale of Brahms' *Fourth Symphony,* there are no subdivisions of the dotted-half pulse in measures 1–8. The composite rhythm beginning at measure 9 divides the dotted half into one third and two thirds. The "missing" third quarter of every measure is implied and then explicitly articulated after measure 16. The absence of any subdivisions of the dotted half in measures 1–8 and of the quarter for quite a way past measure 9 belies the character implied by the tempo marking. As in many other passacaglias and variation forms, the appearance of increasing levels of subdivisions as the movement progresses is a primary factor in the process of growth in this movement.

In Schubert's "Unfinished" (example 3-12), the lone quarter in measure 2 is half the duration of the previous note and one third the duration of the first note. The quarter-note pulse implied in measure 2 is confirmed in measure 4.

All the preceding passages establish at least one clear pulse early in the movement. Some other pieces do not project a clear

Brahms, *Symphony No. 4,* op. 98, fourth movement

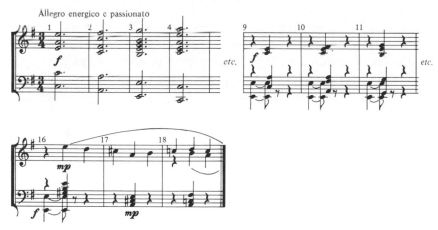

Schubert, *"Unfinished" Symphony,* first movement

3–12

sense of pulse at their openings. This occurs where there are no constant units articulated, as at the opening of Beethoven's *String Quartet,* op. 59, no. 3 (example 3-13), or because tremolos or thick textures do not allow a clear presentation of a pulse (as in example 3-14). At the opening of this Beethoven quartet, the absence of a pulse complements the harmonic and tonal ambiguity. The opening chords are widely separated in time; with no articulated duration during these spans, it is difficult to gather even a precise sense of how long they are. The quarter-note pulse that is established by measure 7 disappears again in measure 8. For the remainder of the introduction, only isolated quarters occur in any part, often widely separated from motions in another part. The result is the otherworldly wandering from one harmony to another without a strong sense of pulse. Similar ambiguity of pulse occurs at the opening of other pieces, especially where the tempo is slow. See the beginning of the prelude to the first act of Wagner's *Tristan und Isolde* for another instance.

At the opening of Beethoven's *Ninth Symphony* (example 3-14), there is a notated unit of counting in the sextuplets. But the indistinction in this figure in most performances and the lack of coordination with the thirty-second upbeats precludes a clear sense of the sextuplet pulse. Among the other figures in this passage, the thirty-second notes are too widely separated to create a strong sense of a pulse. The only regularly recurring units in measures 1–10 are half notes articulated by thirty-second note upbeats. Only as shorter durations subdivide this unit, beginning with measure 11, does a more rapid pulse become established. Thus, the opening of this piece, while nominally in the same tempo and meter as the remainder of the movement, does not sound as if it is. This type of beginning, in which the meter and tempo are notationally the same as in the body of the movement, but in which the pulse is not clearly articulated, was a favorite for many nineteenth-century composers.

Grouping a Pulse

Pulses are grouped on a given level by accentual factors that occur at a slower pace than the pulse itself. Harmonic change is the strongest accentual factor capable of establishing a metric grouping of a pulse. The primacy of harmonic change reflects the importance of harmonic units in tonal music and the clear-cut sense of a point of initiation articulated by a harmonic change.

Meter

3–13. Beethoven, *String Quartet*, op. 59, no. 3, first movement

3–14. Beethoven, *Symphony No. 9*, op. 125, first movement

In example 3-15, the harmonic changes on every half note group the melodic eighth notes in fours. The grouping into fours implies pairing of eighths, a metric level specified in the third measure.

3–15. Schubert, *Symphony No. 5,* fourth movement

Where harmonic changes occur too rapidly or too slowly to group a given pulse, durational and textural accents are the factors that most convincingly provide metric groupings. Textural accents reinforce harmonic changes in example 3-15. Review the opening of Mozart's *Piano Sonata,* K. 545, in example 3-5. Harmonic changes occur every half note, beginning in measure 2. But already in measure 1, textural accents mark off groups of four, then two eighths. Textural accents provide an especially important clarification of metric grouping when a movement begins with an upbeat and there is no harmonic change on the first downbeat (see the excerpts in example 3-16).

Review also the unaccompanied melody in example 3-12 that begins Schubert's "Unfinished" *Symphony.* Any harmonic changes are up to the interpretation of the listener, and with an unaccompanied melody there can be no textural accents. Subdivisions of previously stated durations and later durational accents establish the meter: the half note and the quarter note in measure 2 subdivide the previously established dotted half; and the durational accents in measures 3 and 5 confirm the grouping of quarter notes in threes.

In the opening of Mozart's *Symphony No. 40* in example 3-8, harmonic changes do not begin until measure 5. Prior to that point, textural and durational accents have established several metric lev-

Beethoven, *Piano Sonata,* op. 13, third movement

Beethoven, *Symphony No. 5,* op. 67, first movement

Chopin, *Waltz,* op. 64, no. 2

Bach, *Brandenburg Concerto No. 6,* third movement

3–16

els. The textural accents on each downbeat mark the only points of convergence of the three textural components: the melody, the viola part, and the bass. These textural accents group the viola eighths into groups of eight. The durational accents in the melody articulate quarter notes, grouping the eighths in pairs, and establish metric accentuations every half note.

This passage also illustrates the role of pattern length in projecting metric groupings. A variety of recurring patterns appear here. In the viola part the pairs of eighth notes articulated by pitch changes announce quarter notes even before the appearance of that value in the melody. The low-high patterning supports the half-note level. The ♩♩ | ♩ motive in the melody also projects half notes. The durational accent on the quarter note within this motive occurs on a strong beat. But the pattern-beginning accent consistently occurs on a metrically weak quarter note.

In general in tonal music, pattern length and internal accentuations within a pattern agree with the meter, but the beginning of pattern recurrences may not. Review the discussion of example 2-35, which demonstrates how the disagreement of pattern-beginning and metric accents enlivens the music.

The strength of harmonic change in relation to textural and durational accents is demonstrated by the opening of Brahms' *Symphony No. 1* (review example 3-8). In this passage, all the sustained parts are doubled in several octaves (not shown in example 3-8). Two sets of textural accents occur in each measure: the bass plus the ascending scale in measures 1–4, and the bass plus the descending thirds. Durational accents in the ascending scale mark off further points. Despite these accentuations, it is the harmonic changes over the pedal every three eighths that establish and maintain the metric grouping of eighth notes.

Only in the absence of harmonic changes and durational and textural accents do other features serve to imply metric groupings. Review the very opening of Beethoven's *Violin Sonata*, op. 30, no. 3, in example 3-8. Pattern recurrence, articulation (the six-note slurs), and contour accents are the only applicable features in measure 1. They all agree on the dotted half as an organizer of six sixteenths. Within each six-group, only contour accents apply. These imply a 3 + 3 grouping of sixteenths. Not until measure 2 does the eighth-note pulse make it clear that the sixteenths are grouped into 2 + 2 + 2, not 3 + 3. The harmonic changes in measure 3 confirm the meter.

The weakness of pattern repetition as a metric determinant in comparison to harmonic changes, durational accents, and textural accents, is evident in passages where pattern repetition conflicts with these factors. Listen to example 3-17. The duple grouping implied by the unaccompanied pattern at the opening is immediately superseded when harmonic changes begin.

3–17. Beethoven, *Piano Sonata,* op. 14, no. 2, third movement

Dynamic Stresses. Dynamic stresses are commonly used by performers to emphasize other accentuations. But by themselves in the absence of other accentuations, dynamic stresses are incapable of projecting a metric grouping. A singularly dramatic demonstration of this is the opening of the minuet from Mozart's *String Quartet,* K. 387 (see example 3-18). Although the placement of the downbeat is not asserted unambiguously in measures 1 and 2, pattern length does assert a three-quarter grouping. The dynamic stresses in measures 3–6 do not establish a two-quarter grouping. When the cello continues the stresses in measures 7–8, the harmonic changes unambiguously project the notated meter. The consequent phrase makes merry over any possible metric ambiguity caused by the stresses as they occur unsynchronized in the second violin and viola.

Probably the most telling rebuttal of any meter-producing role of dynamic stresses is the fact that they are totally unnecessary on instruments that are incapable of producing a dynamic stress. The meter of a given piece is just as easily projected on a harpsichord or organ as it is on a piano. Harmonic change, durational accents, and textural accents project quite easily in the absence of dynamic stresses.

3–18. Mozart, *String Quartet*, K. 387, second movement

Meter and Harmonic Change

Harmonic change is the single most powerful meter-producing factor. Paradoxically, there are some passages in which the placement of harmonic changes may be difficult to determine unless the meter is known first. In this type of situation, durational accents may override harmonic changes as factors creating the metric grouping. Listen to the opening of the finale of Haydn's *Piano Sonata in D* (example 3-19). With unaccompanied melody notes on the downbeats of measures 2 and 4, the precise point of harmonic change cannot be determined from pitch alone here. If the accompaniment were more continuous, as in example 3-20, the points of harmonic change would suffice to establish unambiguous metric accents. But without these clear-cut harmonic-change accents, the durational accents are the only factor present to group the eighth-note pulse.

3–19. Haydn, *Piano Sonata*, Hob. XVI/37, third movement

Haydn, *Piano Sonata*, Hob. XVI/37, third movement

3–20

Imagine the excerpt without the durational accents, as in example 3-21. The version below the unbarred excerpt is probably what would project.

3-21

In a passage such as this Haydn excerpt, in which durational accents play the determining role, performers often stress the beats dynamically. This allows the accentuation on the durationally-accented notes to be immediate, even on first hearing (when a listener has no way of knowing which notes are to be longer until they are past). By contrast, such dynamic accents are generally avoided when durational accents support an already established meter. The opening of Mozart's *Fortieth* (example 3-8), which has the same ♫ | ♩ melodic pattern as the Haydn sonata, will not tolerate such dynamic accents. Neither will the opening of Mozart's *Sonata*, K. 545 (example 3-5). Where the meter is already clear from other factors, the durational accents do not need such reinforcement—adding them makes the performance overaccented and plodding.

Summary

Establishing the metric hierarchy of a piece or section involves establishing a pulse and organizing that pulse. Pulses arise from recurring rhythmic values in a single part, in the composite rhythm, or from a regularity that occurs amid other durational patterns. Continuous activity makes palpable every unit of a pulse. But it is not necessary to hear every unit in order to know that these units exist.

Pulses group on the basis of accentuations proceeding at a

slower pace than the pulse itself. Harmonic-change accentuation (harmonic rhythm) is the factor that most easily organizes pulses into a metric level. At levels where harmonic changes do not occur, or where the harmonic rhythm is ambiguous, durational and textural accents are primary factors in establishing the metric level. The lengths of motivic patterns generally agree with the lengths of metric units, but the placement of pattern beginnings often does not. Once several levels of the metric hierarchy have been established, the remaining levels are often inferrable according to the nesting principle.

THE INTERACTION OF METER AND RHYTHMS

With the meter-producing factors clarified, we can now turn to a more comprehensive study of the individual metric-rhythmic structure of several passages starting with example 3-22, Mozart's *Symphony No. 40, K. 550,* first movement. The very opening of Mozart's *Symphony No. 40* presents a metric hierarchy ranging from eighth notes to two-measure units. At every level of the hierarchy, the pulses and the groupings are continually articulated. The eighth-note pulse is grouped into quarters by the patterning in the viola part as well as by the quarter notes and the slurs in the melody. The resulting quarter-note pulse is grouped into half notes by the patterning within the viola part (♪♪♩♩) and the melody (♩ |♩). This half-note pulse is grouped into measure-long units by the bass notes. The measure-long units themselves are grouped in pairs by the harmonic rhythm and by the low-high patterning of the bass part.

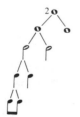

All levels are continually present during the first phrases.

Although all levels technically begin at measure 1, a listener

3–22. Mozart, *Symphony No. 40,* K. 550, first movement

becomes aware of the different levels at different times. During the first measure, the eighth-quarter level is most apparent. This is the level that clearly articulates the *allegro molto* tempo marking. The quarter-half level is apparent immediately from the viola and melody patternings. The larger groupings, especially the two-measure units, become clear only when the listener realizes that amid the haste of the eighths and quarters, the harmonies unfold in a rather relaxed fashion.

Indeed, it is the continual presence of so many different rates of activity that defines some of the magic of the passage. The leisurely harmonic changes occur over the eighth-quarter activity. Or, to put it the other way, all the eighth-quarter activity occurs within a leisurely metric and harmonic frame. There is no harmonic change at all in the first four measures. And when a harmonic progression finally gets underway, it is a tonic-oriented (tonic-prolonging) progression: I II$^4_2$ V$^6_{5-7}$ I. Not until the change in inversion of the dominant in measure 8 does the bass part move from one scale step to another by more than a semitone. Despite the balanced phrases of the melody, this opening is not a period that lays out a number of harmonic goals. Not until measure 15 does the first non-tonic harmonic goal of the movement, the dominant, arrive.

The continual presence of activity on so many levels means that any one of several metric levels might be regarded as a primary metric level. The "allegro molto" designation clearly refers to the eighth-quarter level but is inappropriate for the higher levels.

The great length of the upbeat in the opening melodic motive—five quarter notes, or longer than one notated measure—is one of the factors that seem to mandate that the movement begin with the accompaniment.[4] That way, the complete metric hierarchy is already present by the first true melodic downbeat in measure 3. Later in the movement, when this melody recurs, the entire metric hierarchy is clear because of preceding music, and a complete accompanimental texture does not enter until that first true downbeat. See measures 20–22, 103–105, 164–66, 183–85, and 285–87.

Within the regularity of all these levels, several subtle factors exist that prevent the passage from being as ponderous as some of the analysis above might imply. Within the viola pattern, for instance, the upper notes appear on weak quarter notes, creating a contour or change-of-register accent on weak beats throughout. In the melody, the patterns always begin on weak quarters (♪ ♩|♩), imparting an accent caused by initiation of a pattern to many weak beats. The final note of each phrase subdivision (the first B♭ in measure 3, the second C in measure 5, the first A in measure 7, and the second B♭ in measure 9) occurs on a weak quarter, imparting a durational accent to those beats. In measures 3 and 7, the final quarters receive a contour or change-of-register accent. Finally, throughout the melody, the rhythm of pitch changes often articulates weak subdivisions of the beat.

Some of these factors are rather subtle, and each by itself is perhaps not terribly crucial to the passage. But taken together, they add to the gracefulness and magic that is so much a part of this opening by creating continuities that cross the metrically strong points and emphasize the metrically weak points, but without upsetting the clear metric hierarchy.[5] Just imagine the passage without any of these features (example 3-23):

3–23. "Wolfpack A. Zartlos," *Symphony No. 40*

The second passage to be examined here is Bach's *Prelude in Ab Major (Well-Tempered Clavier,* II [example 3-24]). Like Mozart's *Fortieth,* this prelude establishes a complete metric hierarchy right from the start. Sixteenth-note continuity is maintained from measure 1 until three bars before the end of the composition. Thirty-second-note subdivisions of sixteenths already appear in measure 1 (grouped into pairs since they subdivide previous sixteenths) and grow more numerous as the piece evolves. Sixteenths are grouped into eighths from the beginning of measure 1 by the repeated C/Ab eighth notes (measure 1, beat 1) and the eighth-note alternation between bass and top voice in that measure. The bass pitch motion and durational accents, as well as the repetition of the right-hand patterning every four sixteenths, already group the eighths into quarters during measure 1. The quarters are grouped in threes by the change in pattern occurring every other measure in the first four measures; the dotted halves are grouped in pairs by the harmonic rhythm.

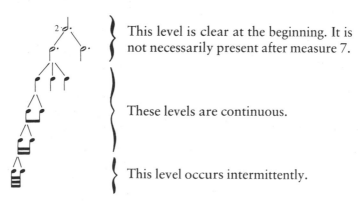

This level is clear at the beginning. It is not necessarily present after measure 7.

These levels are continuous.

This level occurs intermittently.

3–24. Bach, *Prelude in A♭ (Well-Tempered Clavier,* II)

Although this passage is like the opening of Mozart's *Fortieth* in that it presents a complete metric hierarchy, it is unlike the *Fortieth* in the types of activity and the metric levels that draw our attention. In the first movement of the *Fortieth,* the fastest continuous values (eighth notes) are in an accompanimental part, completely regular in patterning. The more leisurely pace of activity in the melody and in the harmonies is more prominent. In Bach's prelude, on the other hand, the activity at the fast levels is not an accompaniment but the foreground. As a result, the eighths, sixteenths, and thirty-seconds introduce a variety of patterns whose accentuations often occur at metrically weak points. In the first and third measures, for instance, the upper-voice syncopations (♪ ♩ ♩ ♪) are reinforced by durational accents created by the right-hand sixteenths. These sixteenths also set up a pattern that appears for much of this excerpt—initiating a motion on the second sixteenth of a beat, especially the second sixteenth of the first beat of a measure. See the voice entries in measures 2, 4, and 6, and the comparable motivic initiations at the beginnings of measures 6–9. After the opening-turn figuration in measure 2 (A♭-G♭-F-G♭), the new motion begins on the second sixteenth of the second beat, a pattern followed in measures 4–9 and elsewhere. In many places following a point of initiation on the second sixteenth of a beat, the ensuing sixteenth receives a registral accent. See, for instance, measure 2, E♭, and measure 4, F.

When thirty-second notes appear more frequently, they often occur in groups of three, beginning on an unaccented thirty-second note (measures 7–15). In the right hand in measures 11–16, durational accents following the thirty-seconds are invariably on weak beat-subdivisions. In the first four of these measures, the following dotted-eighth note gives rise to another durational accent, this time on the weak eighth of a beat. These figures are on the first beats of measures, creating an accentuation off the beat following the strongest metrical point. In these measures (example 3-25) different factors give rise to numerous accentuations.

Even in as seemingly routine a place as the cadential $^6_4$ and dominant that ends measure 16, the right-hand patterning imparts registral accents to the two weak sixteenths. Imagine measures 11–16 without many of these accent-producing features (example 3-26).

The multiplicity of accentual patterns in the fastest pulse levels probably is a primary factor in inducing many performers to take a

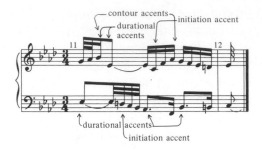

3–25. Bach, *Prelude in A♭ (Well-Tempered Clavier, II)*

3–26. "J. S. Botch," *Prelude in A♭*

rather slow tempo for this prelude. Nearly all recordings take the piece between ♩ = 50 and ♩ = 62, concentrating on the lower levels of the metric hierarchy. Wanda Landowska, in the slowest performance of which I am aware, double-dots most ♪ ♪ figures (such as in measures 5–9), thereby adding additional thirty-second-note activity. This, in addition to the ritardandos she adds at many points, makes perception of higher levels in the metric hierarchy (such as the two-measure units created by the harmonic rhythm at the opening) all but impossible. Glenn Gould takes the opposite approach, and concentrates on the higher metric levels. At his tempo of ♩ = 84, the thirty-second notes go by too fast to be perceived individually, but the two-measure units are clearly projected, and even higher levels seem to be hinted at.

That such divergent tempos are possible is the result of the full activity at all levels of the metric hierarchy. This prelude has been recorded at tempos that vary by 68 percent, in contrast to the first movement of Mozart's *Fortieth,* where recordings by conductors as diverse as Beecham, Böhm, Britten, Casals, Davis, Hogwood, Klemperer, Szell, and Toscanini differ by only 21 percent.

Our third example of rhythmic-metric structure is Beethoven's *Symphony No. 5,* op. 67, first movement (example 3-27). Like the Mozart and Bach passages just discussed, the opening of Beethoven's *Fifth* lays out, at least by implication, a full metric hierarchy. The eighth-note pulse and the durationally-accented final note of the opening motive are present right from the opening. When the continuous music, uninterrupted by fermatas, begins in measure 6, the eighths are grouped in fours on the basis of durational accents and accents caused by pattern beginnings. The harmonic changes in measures 11 and 15–21 confirm this grouping. The half notes are themselves grouped into fours on the basis of the harmonies in measures 7 and 11. When patterns repeat every two measures, beginning on the upbeat to measure 15, these four-measure units are subdivided into twos.

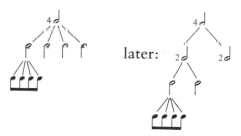

What is significantly different about this beginning in relation to that of Mozart's *Fortieth* or Bach's A♭-*Prelude* is that various in-

3–27. Beethoven, *Symphony No. 5,* op. 67, first movement

termediate levels in the metric hierarchy are present only by implication at first. The grouping of half notes in pairs occurs only as a
subdivision of the already established four-half grouping. And
grouping of eighths into pairs does not arise until the articulations
of measures 38–43. (See example 2-15.) Other than a single
quarter-note woodwind chord in measure 51, there is no quarter-
note activity at all until the second theme group, which by contrast
features extensive quarter-note motion.

With the absence of any quarter-note activity to group the
eighths in pairs and the absence of any factors at first that might
group the half notes in pairs, the eighths and halves at the opening
are each grouped in fours. One might well imagine that measures 6–
21 were notated in $\frac{4}{4}$, with the short values being sixteenths (example 3-28). Indeed, such a notation is plausible for many passages in
the movement. It is only because the half notes of Beethoven's notation are occasionally grouped in three pairs (six measures) or even
in odd numbers (three or five measures) that the movement had to
be notated in $\frac{2}{4}$, with the half note or notated measure being a single
pulse at the primary metric level. The notation in example 3-28, if
continued for the entire movement, would have necessitated notated changes in meter. (See example 3-36)[6]

3–28

Several examples in chapter 2 note the effect of pattern-
beginning and pitch-change accents that articulate the second
eighth of many measures at the opening of the symphony. It is the
rapid eighth-note pulse, consistently accenting the second eighth of
the measure, within the otherwise undivided half notes grouped in
fours that creates the strong rhythmic propulsion of this passage
and, indeed, of much of the movement. Unlike Bach's A♭-Prelude,
in which many accentual patterns define each unit of pulse at sev-

eral levels, or Mozart's *Fortieth*, in which a fully articulated metric hierarchy measures movement, Beethoven's *Fifth* emphasizes large-scale motions over a rapid pulse.

The metric accentuations on the downbeat and the persistent accentuations on the second eighth of the measure give rise to a rhythmic focus and power quite different from that found in the Bach or Mozart examples. Imagine how much less driven this music would sound if an accompaniment were present that would complete the metric hierarchy, thereby adding more accentuations and diluting the accentual focus of Beethoven's version (example 3-29).

3–29

MAINTAINING A METER

Once a metric hierarchy has been established, we, as listeners, will maintain that organization as long as minimal evidence is present, even in the face of accentual factors that would give rise to a different metric structure in the absence of such an imposed meter. In addition, accentual features which by themselves would not be able to establish a metric grouping can often serve to maintain an already established meter.

Consider, for instance, the opening of Brahms' *First Symphony* (example 3-30). We have already discussed the factors that group the eighths in threes at the opening. (Review the discussion of example 3-8.) After the downbeat of measure 9, most factors until measure 12 point to a grouping of eighths in threes, starting on the second eighth of the notated measure. But when we hear this passage following the preceding music, in which the strong eighth-note pulse was grouped in threes, the continuing eighth pulse in measures 9–12 insures the maintenance of the notated grouping. Lest any doubts remain, Brahms notated the crescendo-diminuendo placement in measures 11–12 to confirm the proper metric accents.

3–30. Brahms, *Symphony No. 1,* op. 68, first movement

Dynamics, normally a secondary factor in creating a meter, here reinforce an already existent meter. In measure 12 and again after measure 16, the harmonic changes confirm the notated meter.

Of course, the ability of a listener to continue the previous meter through measures 9–12 depends in part on the performance.

78

Some conductors pause between the first two eighths of measure 9, probably to set off the new section and to allow the forte chord to finish resonating before the softer music begins. When such a break lasts close to or even more than an eighth note, any sense of metric continuity may be destroyed.

Once a meter has been established, its power is so great that it can overrule the actual occurrence of a harmonic change and have us interpret that change as either an anticipation or a delay (resulting from a suspension) of the "actual" point of change.

See measures 9–16 from the finale of Brahms' *Symphony No. 4* in example 3-31. Harmonic changes and durational accents in the composite rhythm mark off the second notated beat of each measure. But following the eight undivided dotted halves of measures 1–8, the notated meter remains clear throughout measures 9–16.

3–31. Brahms, *Symphony No. 4*, op. 98, fourth movement

Listen also to the excerpt from the opening of Schumann's *Faschingsschwank aus Wien* (example 3-32). The notated meter at the opening is established by harmonic changes, durational accents, and pattern repetitions. Within this meter, the upbeat to measure 5 is clearly an anticipation of the harmonic change "due" on the downbeat of measure 5. (The upbeat to measure 1 is unaffected. On first hearing, we have not yet established a meter. When the repeat is taken, there is no harmonic change. Only on returns of this section in the rondo movement does the upbeat to measure 1 sound like a harmonic anticipation of the following downbeat.) The same

3–32. Schumann, *Faschingsschwank aus Wien*, op. 26, first movement

elements affect the upbeats to measures 9 and 17. In measures 10 and 12, the opposite effect is present. The rest in the bass marks the "missing" root of the chord over which the right-hand part is suspended. The upbeat anticipations of this passage are a motivation for the second trio section of the movement, part of which appears in example 2-6. Occasional downbeats in this trio confirm the notated meter. Later sections of the movement continue to explore such suppressed downbeats in other ways.

Isolating excerpts from their context has led some theorists to raise questions about the meter of otherwise unambiguous passages. One such passage, from Mozart's *Piano Quartet in G Minor,* K. 478 (example 3-33), was cited by Arnold Schoenberg in his essay "Brahms the Progressive" as an instance of changing meter.[7] Schoenberg does not cite the criteria for his rebarring. The revision seems to be based on durational accents and, in part, on the point at which Schoenberg interprets harmonic changes to take place. Cone disagrees with Schoenberg's revision, arguing that the meter is entirely regular here, with functional downbeats on the middle of each notated measure. The nonharmonic tones on several chord changes are the complicating factors.[8]

But neither Schoenberg nor Cone, nor most of the other theorists that have discussed this passage,[9] sets this music in its context. The metric hierarchy has been firmly established for many measures before the appearance of this theme. The accompaniment in measures 57–64 maintains the eighth-note, quarter-note, and half-note pulses. As in the Brahms excerpts in examples 3-30 and 3-31, the factors in this passage do not destroy the established meter—they merely add to it other accentual patterns. And as in Schumann's *Faschingsschwank aus Wien* (example 3-32), the previous meter makes clear that certain harmonic changes are early or late because of nonharmonic tones.

Consider also the first movement of Brahms' *Violin Concerto.* The movement is in $\frac{3}{4}$, but contains several passages in which quarter notes are grouped in fives by patterning. In all these cases, the excerpt is both preceded and followed by music unambiguously in triple meter. The five-beat groupings are accentual patterns in contrast to the $\frac{3}{4}$ meter, not a change of meter (see example 3-34). In measures 53–57, the even quarters and the lack of internal articulation, following the preceding music, do not destroy the $\frac{3}{4}$ meter.

The following instance of five-beat groupings, in measures

Schoenberg's perception of the metric structure:

or:

3–33. Mozart, *Piano Quartet*, K. 478, first movement

3–34. Brahms, *Violin Concerto*, op. 77, first movement

69–72, is more pronounced. But even here, the lack of harmonic change weakens any establishment of a new meter. Instead, the pattern seems to migrate across the meter until, by measure 73, the long note has arrived on the downbeat. For the remainder of the passage, the durational accents support the notated meter.

In measures 300–303, the harmonic changes remain in $\frac{3}{4}$ and cut across any five-beat patternings (example 3-35). The lack of harmonic changes in measures 304–306 undercuts any possible change. When the bass does begin to move in measure 307, it is always in $\frac{3}{4}$.

3–35. Brahms, *Violin Concerto*, op. 77, first movement

Although all of these excerpts involve accentual patterns in opposition to the meter, they do not contain true metric ambiguity, and certainly not metric change at the quarter-half or quarter-dotted-half level. For an instance of metric change, listen to example 3-36.

Measures 362 through 388 are grouped in fours (or pairs of two) on the basis of harmonic changes, durational accents, texture, and pattern repetition. After measure 399, the groupings in four continue. But this meter cannot be maintained through the intervening music. There are *nine* measures from 390–98—somewhere (exactly where is open to debate) there must be a five-measure grouping. This is a true metric change, unlike any of the other excerpts discussed here.[10]

3–36. Beethoven, *Symphony No. 5*, op. 67, first movement

4

METRIC AMBIGUITY AND CHANGE

The last section of chapter 3 presents a number of passages in which patterns of accentuation are in conflict with a meter without upsetting that meter. Although in general an already existing meter will not be easily destroyed, there are indeed situations in which metric ambiguity does arise. These situations occur primarily when a meter is being established (namely, at the beginning of a movement or after an unmeasured pause) and when conflicting patterns of accentuation persist and upset an already established meter.

When metric ambiguity occurs at the opening of a movement or after a fermata or other unmeasured pause, it arises either from conflicting criteria of accentuation or from a lack of sufficient accentuations to establish a given metric level. The listener either receives conflicting signals or insufficient signals to establish the metric hierarchy. Of quite a different nature is metric ambiguity occurring in a continuous passage after a meter has already been established. In this case, a listener may well continue to organize the music according to the preceding meter even in the face of persistent cross-accentuations. Only when a decisive shift in meter-producing accentuations—that is, a metric change—takes place, or when meter-producing accentuations become so irregular that any patterning becomes difficult, will metric ambiguity and, perhaps, a change to a new metric order occur. Because of the differences between metric ambiguity as a meter is being established and metric ambiguity leading to a change of meter, I will discuss each of these separately.

METRIC AMBIGUITY AS A METER IS BEING ESTABLISHED

In a strict sense, there is metric ambiguity at the opening of all movements and after all unmeasured pauses. The listener must use the accentuations within the very opening music to establish at least part of the metric hierarchy. But in most movements, the signals are clear enough that the establishment of the metric hierarchy occurs in the straightforward manner described in chapter 3. In some cases, however, the process cannot be so straightforward. The opening of the slow movement of Mozart's "Jupiter" *Symphony* is a case in point (see example 4-1). Several levels of the metric hierarchy are unambiguous in this passage. A quarter-note pulse is clear from the beginning. (Review the discussion of example 3-10). Subdivisions of this pulse become clearer as the melody continues. But above this level there is ambiguity. Grosvenor Cooper and Leonard Meyer, as well as Wallace Berry, have raised questions concerning the grouping of this quarter-note pulse.[1] Harmonic changes on the downbeats of measures 2 and 4 support the notated meter, and, beginning in measure 7, harmonic changes occur on every downbeat. But during the first six measures, several factors strongly emphasize the second beat of these measures. In measures 1–5, there are durational accents on the notated second beat of each measure, supported in measures 2 and 4 by strong textural and dynamic accents. In measure 6, a harmonic and textural change occurs on the notated second beat.

Apparently because of these accentuations, Cooper and Meyer suggest, but immediatcly reject, a duple meter for measures

4–1. Mozart, *Symphony No. 41*, K. 551, second movement

1–6, with the first beat as an upbeat (see example 4-2). In this metric hierarchy, the durational accents of Mozart's measures 1, 3, and 5, and all the harmonic changes occur on downbeats. In rejecting this possibility, Cooper and Meyer assert that "a *latent* duple meter is very strong in these first measures." But for two reasons they argue in favor of Mozart's notated meter. First, they note that the rhythmic structure of Mozart's version is that of a sarabande, with an accented second beat. Second, the structure of the principal ascending melodic motion (A in measure 1, B♭ in measures 2–3, C in measure 4, and D in measure 7) works best if the A, B♭, and C are "stressed weak beats which seek to become accents,"[2] creating a sense of upbeat that is sustained until the arrival on D in measure 7. Cooper and Meyer argue that if the A, B♭, and C were all on downbeats, as in example 4-2, the D would seem an anticlimax rather than a goal.

Both arguments beg the question and are inadequate as explanations for the establishment of a meter and our perception of it. If we, as listeners, learned to hear the passage in $\frac{2}{4}$, why would we ever imagine that it might be a sarabande if we heard it in $\frac{3}{4}$? Similarly, we could never imagine that the A, B♭, and C are "stressed weak beats which seek to become accents" unless we already heard the piece in $\frac{3}{4}$. Cooper and Meyer's argument is predicated on the assumption that we perceive meter in a passage by trying different metric hierarchies and comparing the subtle interpretive advantages of each.[3] Such an approach is implausible. According to their argument, many a phrase in duple meter beginning with an upbeat could be a triple-meter sarabande, and many a straightforward passage could be made quite a bit more interesting by imposing another meter.

Berry argues that the passage is indeed in triple meter, but that in measures 1–5, the true downbeat is the second beat—"a triple meter which is temporarily displaced in relation to the notated bar-line. Only harmonic rhythm accords with the notated bar-line *(establishing a subtle countergrouping)*." His reasons are the accent-

4–2. Cooper and Meyer, *The Rhythmic Structure of Music*, example 102.

producing factors on the second beat of each of measures 1–6 (example 4-3).

4–3. Berry, *Structural Functions in Music,* metric analysis, example 3–9.

But harmonic change is not so easily dismissed here as a factor. Berry's barring insists that the dominant at the end of measure 1 and the tonic at the end of measure 3 are separate from the following downbeats. Since harmonic rhythm is such a crucial factor in establishing a meter, and since continuity within a single harmony is such a fundamental aspect of tonality, Berry's meter could only be projected in performance with a pronounced break between measures 1 and 2 and between measures 3 and 4—a break that I find disruptive to the continuity of the larger phrase. For these Mozart measures are not at all like measures 10 and 12 of Schumann's *Faschingsschwank aus Wien* (review example 3-32). Those Schumann measures, like Berry's version of Mozart in example 4-3, seem to feature the arrival on a harmony during a measure and then the continuation of that harmony into the next measure. But as discussed in connection with example 3-32, the arrival on the C and G chords in measures 10 and 12 of the Schumann passage is delayed from the downbeat by suspensions and a suppressed downbeat. In Berry's version of Mozart's phrase, I find no reason to hear that the V_3^4 (measure 1 in example 4-3) and I_6 (measure 3 in example 4-3) are delayed from the downbeats of those measures.

It is indisputable that there are two regular patterns of accentuation at the opening of the Mozart movement, one pattern caused by the harmonic rhythm, coinciding with the notated downbeats, and the other pattern caused by the durational, dynamic, and textural accents that all coincide with the notated second beats. This passage would be quite different without one or the other of these patterns of accentuation, as suggested by the revisions in example 4-4. Since both patterns are integral to the passage, it seems more in accord with the passage to recognize the presence and interaction of both instead of attempting to explain away one or the other of these accentuations. There is a meter that does agree with the notated

4—4

barring. And there are factors that create strong second-beat accents throughout. This perspective does not insist on ignoring or denigrating any factor(s) but recognizes the role of each factor and the interaction of all the factors in producing the rhythm of the passage.

I have been discussing the meter and accentuations as they stand in the score. When we turn our attention to a listener's perception of the meter, additional factors arise to support the notated meter. A listener hearing the symphony for the first time might be confused about which accentual pattern is *the* meter in measures 1–6. But since later appearances of this theme are straightforward metrically, a listener will.soon learn the notated meter. After four metrically unambiguous measures (7–10), a new version of the opening theme occurs, illustrated in example 4-5.

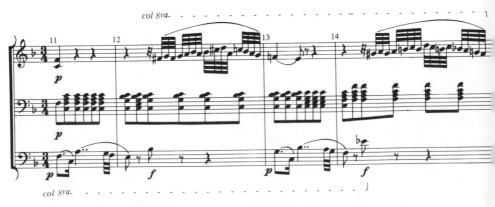

4–5. Mozart, *Symphony No. 41*, K. 551, second movement

Following measures 7–10, with their clear triple meter agreeing with the notated barlines, with a continuous eighth-note pulse, with harmonic changes on the notated downbeats, with a durational accent in the violins on measure 13, and with the accompanying parts unaffected by the dynamic accents in measures 12 and 14, the recurrence of the opening theme is unambiguously in the notated meter. The same factors make clear the notated triple meter at the recapitulation (measures 60 and following). As a result, even the first-time listener will have the notated metric structure firmly reinforced at several points in the movement. When he or she listens to the piece on future occasions, the remembered passages from later in the movement will affect the metric patterning at the opening. This being such a well-known piece, hardly anyone experienced in music comes to it as a naive listener. This fact is recognized by Berry, who prefaces his remarks on this piece by asking us to forget "that we know the piece and its notation and ultimate metric order." His mode of hearing the passage will at best affect only an occasional listener until he or she has heard the entire movement.

Because of the potential for ambiguity at the very opening, performers might well wish to assist the notated meter by emphasizing, perhaps with a slight dynamic accent, the downbeats of measures 1–5. And they might well wish to avoid strong stresses on the second beat in measures 1 and 3. As in other passages we have already discussed, and others we will encounter, the best interpretation here may be to avoid insisting on a single structuring, thereby allowing the full interaction of all patterns to project.

Another opening passage with an ambiguous metric structure, but one which, unlike the Mozart example, retains its potential for ambiguity even on later hearings, is the first movement of Beethoven's *Piano Sonata,* op. 14, no. 2 (see example 4-6). Below the quarter-note level, the metric hierarchy is clear. The sixteenth-note pulse is continuous; and grouping of sixteenths in pairs is already implied by the melodic patterning on the upbeat. And the textural accents caused by the entry of the bass specify which note of the pairs is metrically stronger.

But above this level, there is little clear evidence supporting a metric grouping of eighths or quarters before measure 5. Durational and textural accents favor the second eighth of the notated measures as a downbeat. Contour accents (on the high D's and E's) favor the eighth upbeat of the notated measures as a downbeat. No factor favors the notated downbeat. Harmonic change is of no as-

4–6. Beethoven, *Piano Sonata,* op. 14, no. 2, first movement

sistance because deciding on the point of harmonic change means deciding on the number of upbeat sixteenths, and determining the number of upbeat sixteenths depends on locating the precise point of harmonic change. What is clear from the measure-long pattern repetitions and sequences is that eight sixteenths make a half-note grouping. But that does not specify the location of metric accents within this pattern.

Later occurrences of the theme are not very helpful in determining the meter either. Relatively long rhythmic values and the lack of a subdividing pulse at the end of the exposition predispose many performers to end the exposition with a sufficient ritardando so that the repeat of the exposition begins without a clear metric frame. The same situation occurs at the beginning of the development, which starts with the opening material in the minor mode. And both the recapitulation and the false recapitulation (measures 99 and following) begin after fermatas. Only during the development section does the opening motive appear in an unambiguous metric setting in agreement with the notation (measures 81 and following).

Without the strong intervention of the performer (via a pronounced dynamic accentuation or lengthening of the downbeat sixteenth), either of the versions in example 4-7 is easily heard in preference to the notated meter. Even when a listener knows the piece and its notation well, one or the other of these versions can easily seduce him or her. In either version, the music gradually converges

4–7

on the notated meter by measure 8. The bass, which begins its activity on the eighth after the notated barline in measures 1–4, moves to a sixteenth after the notated barline in measures 5–7 and confirms the notated meter beginning in measure 8.

In many passages involving metric ambiguity, such as those just discussed, the ambiguity arises from too many factors pointing to different metric possibilities. But in some passages there is too little information to set up a meter. At the very opening of works like Wagner's *Das Rheingold* or *Siegfried,* too few accentuations are present for a clear pulse or meter to be established. (Also review the opening of Beethoven's *String Quartet,* op. 59, no. 3, in example 3-13.) Indeed, many slow movements are somewhat ambiguous at their openings because of the amount of time it takes for a clear pulse and grouping to be perceived.

But even where a clear pulse is present, the absence of any subdivisions or definitive groupings can create ambiguity. The unbroken succession of dotted halves for the first eight measures of the finale of Brahms' *Fourth Symphony* raises numerous questions about the meter. (Review example 3-31.) Are the dotted halves the pulses of a slow movement? Or are they larger groupings in a fast movement?

Structural Effects of Metric Ambiguity

The opening of a piece can be metrically ambiguous to foreshadow cross-accentuations in later passages. At the very opening of Schumann's *"Rhenish" Symphony,* for instance, the 2 + 2 + 2 organization of quarter notes appears three times before the 3 + 3 organization. These patterns follow one another and occur simultaneously at many points in the movement (example 4-8).

A somewhat similar situation arises at the beginning of Brahms' *Third Symphony.* But here metric ambiguity is maintained

4–8. Schumann, *Symphony No. 3,* op. 97, first movement

on several levels. Not until the conclusion of the first harmonic motion away from and back to the tonic does the notated $^6_4$ meter become clear (example 4-9).

The measure unit is specified in the first two measures. The
first subdivision of this unit, in the melody in measures 3–6, is into
three half notes. Although the quarters and eighths in the accompaniment may not be easily discernible in performance, the ♩. ♪ and ♩♩
figures in the melody specify the duple subdivisions at the half- and
quarter-note level. Durational accents in the melody support the
changes of harmony on each downbeat in reinforcing the measure
length. But no factors other than the melodic subdivisions support
the $^3_2$ meter. In measures 7–8, the harmonic rhythm and durational
accents in the melody support a dotted-half subdivision of the measure. If $^3_2$ was assumed in measures 3–6, it will hardly survive measures 7–8. The sequential continuation in measures 9–10 seems at
first to confirm the $^6_4$ subdivision of the measure. The melody is
plausible in $^6_4$. But the harmonies in measure 10 revert to an apparent $^3_2$. In measures 11–12, the melody again seems to be in $^6_4$. But the
delay of the harmonic changes until the second quarter of each

dotted-half unit, along with harmonic common tones in the melody at the beginning of each dotted half, fails to reestablish the meter decisively. Not until measures 13–14 is the $\frac{6}{4}$ meter crystal clear.

The gradual metric evolution from ambiguity, change, and forced reinterpretation into clarity conforms with the harmonic structure of the passage. The opening measures freely interchange

4–9. Brahms, *Symphony No. 3*, op. 90, first movement

4–9. (Continued)

major and minor mode, foreshadowing the modal inflections that affect many passages in the entire symphony. (Even on the largest level, the outer movements are in F major and F minor; the middle movements are in C major and C minor.) The first nontonic harmonic goal is the dominant in measure 7—the occasion for the first appearance of $\frac{6}{4}$. The metric confusion of measure 10 parallels the harmonic shift as the prolonged tonic of measures 9–10 turns out not to be a tonic at all but a dominant of IV. Only as the major mode is confirmed in the repeated cadence figure of measures 13–14 is the meter clarified.

Throughout this movement, there are numerous metric complexities that derive from elements in this opening. When the opening material reappears, it is often with the metric ambiguities retained. At the very end of the development, for instance, the melody of measures 3–6 returns in a clear $\frac{3}{2}$ context (measures 112–119 [example 4-10]). The dotted-half subdivisions of measures 120–23 color perception of the following measures more in favor of $\frac{6}{4}$ than does the comparable passage at the opening of the movement. Metrically, the passage from measures 124–36 is identical with measures 3–15. Only in measure 186 and at the very end of the movement does the ♩♩♩.♪ pattern occur against another voice that articulates a $\frac{6}{4}$ pattern. (See example 4-11.)

4–10. Brahms, *Symphony No. 3*, op. 90, first movement

4–11. Brahms, *Symphony No. 3,* op. 90, first movement

METRIC AMBIGUITY LATER IN A MOVEMENT

The preceding excerpts demonstrate metric ambiguity at the opening of movements. Whether or not this ambiguity is resolved by later passages, it is to some extent affected by later passages in the movement. As a listener becomes more familiar with the piece, these passages from later in the movement can affect perception of the beginnings.

In other compositions, metric ambiguity during a movement can be clarified by earlier passages. Consider the first movement of Haydn's "Quinten" *Quartet,* op. 76, no. 2. At the beginning of the coda to the movement, the passage in example 4-12 occurs after a

4–12. Haydn, *String Quartet*, op. 76, no. 2, first movement fermata. Isolated from their context, at least measures 139 and 140 seem to be in a metric structure, an eighth-note off in relation to the notated downbeats. As in some other ambiguous excerpts, the point at which a listener perceives the harmonic changes to take place depends on the placement of the beats—and the placement of the beats depends on the placement of harmonic changes. (Review the discussion of Haydn's *D-Major Piano Sonata* in examples 3-19 through 3-21, and the discussion of Beethoven's *Piano Sonata,* op. 14, no. 2, in examples 4-6 and 4-7.)

In the "Quinten" *Quartet,* several passages earlier in the movement lay out the components that participate in the ambiguous passage in measures 139 and following. The syncopated figures in the accompaniment in measures 139–40 first appear in measures 27 and 30–31. Both measures are preceded and followed by metrically clear music. When the syncopations first recur in the recapitulation (measures 116–17), they are once again prepared and followed by metrically clear music. Their second appearance in the recapitulation (measures 124–25)—their fourth occurrence in the movement—is followed by metrically clear music, but is preceded by a fermata. The sixteenth turns in the first violin in measures 139–40 appear first at the end of the exposition (measures 52–56) in a metrically clear setting.

So when the coda begins, ample precedent has been set for the passage. Though a novice might be startled, a listener experienced with the piece can easily follow the notated metric structure.

Metric Ambiguity and the Listener

It should be clear by this point that some aspects of metric ambiguity are embedded in musical structures, but other, perhaps more important aspects reside in the listener's perception of a passage. Several instances of ambiguity introduced here occur at the beginning of a movement. When we hear the piece for the first time, we may be confused as to the meter, or we may assume a meter that turns out not to be the meter of the remainder of the movement. Even on this first hearing, what do we make of a later passage that clarifies the metric structure of the opening? Does this later passage cause us to recall the earlier one and change its metric structure retroactively? Suppose there is a repeat (as in a sonata-form exposition) and we hear that ambiguous passage again—repeated literally. We now know at least the essence of the later metrical structure. How does this affect our perception?

As we become more and more familiar with the piece, we eventually reach the point at which we anticipate events in that piece (the next note in the melody, the next phrase, harmonies, and so forth) before and as they actually occur. Do the ambiguities recede from our awareness as we impose a meter on the piece? At the very opening of Schumann's "Rhenish" *Symphony* (example 4-8) or the Brahms *Third Symphony* (example 4-9), for instance, a listener well-versed in these pieces may easily hear the music in the notated meter ($\frac{3}{4}$ and $\frac{6}{4}$, respectively) simply by imposing that meter on the music. Is that listener aware any longer that there is no evidence creating dotted-half groupings? If indeed our perception of the piece changes under the effects of memory and anticipation, how can we hope to study such effects? What assertions can we make about the rhythmic or metric structure of a passage that will accord with all the ways the passage might be perceived by a single listener as he or she gets to know the piece? Or should we ignore the naive listener and only analyze according to the perceptions of one familiar with the piece, ignoring how one achieves that understanding, and what sense (or nonsense?) the piece might make to one who never learns it well enough to process it in the so-called sophisticated manner?

Rather than cite questions like these as nearly insurmountable obstacles to the study of meter (or, for that matter, of any aspect of music), I would argue that the changes in perspective gained by our increasing familiarity with a piece of music are part of our increasing appreciation of that piece. These changes are part of what transforms an ambiguous, puzzling, or even confusing and disorienting passage into a familiar one, friendly and beloved. For such changes in perspective affect all aspects of a piece, not only rhythm and meter. In one passage it might be a seemingly peculiar turn of phrase, in another an inexplicable succession of harmonies, a strange simultaneity, or an incomprehensible change of timbre. Perhaps nowhere in the theoretical and aesthetic literature on music is there as sensitive and perceptive a discussion of the way a piece changes with increasing familiarity as in Marcel Proust's *In A Budding Grove*.

But often one listens and hears nothing, if it is a piece of music at all complicated to which one is listening for the first time. And yet when, later on, this sonata had been played over to me two or three times I found that I

101

knew it quite well. And so it is not wrong to speak of hearing a thing for the first time. If one had indeed, as one supposes, received no impression from the first hearing, the second, the third would be equally 'first hearings' and there would be no reason why one should understand it any better after the tenth. Probably what is wanting, the first time, is not comprehension but memory. For our memory, compared to the complexity of the impressions which it has to face while we are listening, is infinitesimal. . . . Of these multiple impressions our memory is not capable of furnishing us with an immediate picture. But that picture gradually takes shape. . . . And not only does one not seize at once and retain an impression of works that are really great, but even in the content of any such work (as befell me in the case of Vinteuil's sonata) it is the least valuable parts that one at first perceives. Thus it was that I was mistaken not only in thinking that this work held nothing further in store for me. . . . When the least obvious beauties of Vinteuil's sonata were revealed to me, those that I had from the first distinguished and preferred in it were beginning to escape, to avoid me. Since I was able only in successive moments to enjoy all the pleasures that this sonata gave me, I never possessed it in its entirety. . . . In Vinteuil's sonata the beauties that one discovers at once are those also of which one most soon grows tired. . . . But when those first apparitions have withdrawn, there is left for our enjoyment some passage which its composition, too new and strange to offer anything but confusion to our mind, had made indistinguishable and so preserved intact. . . . And we shall love it longer than the rest because we have taken longer to get to love it.[4]

The core of Proust's argument is that one is "able only in successive moments to enjoy all the pleasures" that music imparts and that one can never possess it in its entirety. This passage is one of many in his work that argue for the impossibility of experiencing any aspect of life to its fullest as it happens, since the import of that experience cannot be perceived as it happens. Leaving aside such larger issues, I can accept Proust's argument about music until just before his conclusion. In terms of meter and rhythm, a listener does perceive a previously ambiguous passage differently once familiarity has clarified that ambiguity. But the aspects that gave rise to the ambiguity do not evaporate. They remain as a part of the rhythm of the passage—rhythm here used in its broadest sense.

Admittedly, once we know the "Rhenish" or Brahms' *Third*, we may well hear them in dotted-half groupings right from their opening measures. But we do this by adding a metric hierarchy that must always conflict with the accent-producing features in these passages. In chapter 3, I discussed the interaction of factors that create the rhythm at the openings of Mozart's *Fortieth* and Bach's *A♭*

Prelude. It is beyond any listener's capacity to grasp all the aspects of either piece on first hearing. Only as we become more familiar with the pieces can we learn to relish the subtle factors that add life throughout the whole metric hierarchy of Mozart's *Fortieth* or to respond to all the accentuations that energize the faster levels of the metric hierarchy in Bach's A♭ *Prelude.* Nevertheless, in a passage that is at first metrically ambiguous, learning to hear it in the meter of the preceding or following unambiguous passages does not diminish the effect of the ambiguity—rather it heightens this effect since the ambiguous structures now coexist with the imposed meter.

METRIC CHANGE

At Faster Levels in the Metric Hierarchy. Temporary or permanent changes in the grouping or subdivision of a pulse can happen at any level in the metric hierarchy. At lower metric levels, changes in the subdivision of a pulse are common. Eighths and sixteenths subdividing quarters may change to eighth-triplets. When such changes occur within a phrase, they affect the composite rhythm by increasing or decreasing rates of activity. In example 4-13, for instance, the introduction of triplets approaching the cadence allows an increase in the level of activity without either the doubling of motion that an introduction of sixteenths would produce or the uneven flow that an eighth plus two sixteenths would produce.

Changes in beat subdivisions often serve an additional formal function when they happen between phrases or sections, differentiating portions of a movement from one another. Instances of this

4-13. Beethoven, *Violin Sonata*, op. 30, no. 2, first movement

103

occur in all periods of tonal music. In Bach's *Chaconne* from the *D Minor Partita for Violin Alone,* sextuplet variations occur as a group, distinguished from other variations featuring sixteenths or thirty-seconds. In the first movement of Mozart's *String Quartet,* K. 421, sextuplets occur late in the exposition and recapitulation, following the sixteenths earlier in the second theme group. The first half of the slow movement of Beethoven's "Pathétique" *Sonata,* op. 13, has continuous sixteenths; the second half of the movement features continuous sextuplets. In the first movement of Brahms' *Fourth Symphony,* quarter-note triplets in the second theme group contrast with only duple divisions in the first theme group.[5]

Although changes in the subdivisions of a constant beat are common, changes in the grouping of rapid pulses are virtually unknown in tonal music. The alternation of $\frac{2}{4}$, $\frac{3}{4}$, and $\frac{3}{8}$ in the *Soldier's March,* and of $\frac{2}{4}$, $\frac{3}{4}$, $\frac{3}{8}$, $\frac{5}{8}$, $\frac{7}{8}$, and $\frac{7}{16}$ in the *Music to Scene 1* in Stravinsky's *L'Histoire du Soldat* have no substantive predecessors in tonal literature.[6]

At the Primary Metric Level. At higher levels in the metric hierarchy, pulses often do regroup to form larger units of differing lengths. Listen to the excerpt from Mahler's *Symphony No. 4* in example 4-14. The music preceding this excerpt is in a somewhat faster tempo but clearly in a duple meter (as is all the music thus far in the movement). The grouping of quarters in measures 38–40 is in pairs because of harmonic changes and textural accents, reinforced by durational accents in the melody. In measure 41, this grouping is disrupted. Beginning with measure 42, the duple meter resumes. The parallelism of measures 42–44 with measures 38–39, along with all the other factors that impart a duple grouping of quarters, beginning in measure 42, ensures the reestablishment of the duple meter. Mahler's metric notation reflects the change in metric grouping in measure 41.

Regrouping of pulses to form measures of different lengths, as in Mahler's *Symphony No. 4,* is common in eighteenth- and nineteenth-century music. What is uncharacteristic of even the late nineteenth century in this Mahler excerpt is that the change is reflected in the meter signature and that it occurs in a lyrical passage in a moderately slow tempo. In earlier music, metric changes of this sort occur mostly in scherzos and in other fast movements in which the notated measure is a single beat (as in the first movement of Beethoven's *Fifth*).[7] Such changes will be discussed shortly.

4–14. Mahler, *Symphony No. 4*, first movement

Other instances of changed groupings at the primary metric level occur in those rare instances of quintuple or septuple meter, in which the primary metric level alternates between duple and triple groupings. For quintuple meter, see the second movement of Tchaikovsky's "Pathétique" *Symphony* (in which the harmonic rhythm underscores the divisions in some measures, while others are ambiguous), and act 3, scene 2, from Wagner's *Tristan und Isolde*. The $\frac{5}{4}$ passages (measures 31–32, 62–63, *passim*) are based on transformations of an earlier theme in triple meter. Indeed, almost all the metric changes in act 3, scene 2, feature alterations in previously stated themes. This, together with harmonic rhythm, makes the changes immediately perceptible. These changes and transformations of previous material reflect Tristan's state of delirium.

Brahms' *Variations on a Hungarian Song*, op. 21, no. 2, features a $\frac{7}{4}$ meter (notated $\frac{3}{4}$C) in the theme and in the first eight variations. But the notated meter may not be the perceived meter in many measures because of different accent-producing factors.

The $\frac{4}{4}$-$\frac{3}{4}$-$\frac{4}{4}$ alternation in Mahler's *Symphony No. 4* (example 4-15) is a grouping change at the primary metric level. The $\frac{4}{4}$-$\frac{2}{4}$-$\frac{4}{4}$ change in the same excerpt (measures 42–44) affects the next higher level. This type of change is very common in duple meter in all tonal styles. Although Mahler notates the shift here (caused by the expansion of the melody B-A from quarter notes in measure 39 to half notes in measure 44), many other composers simply allow the shift to take place within $\frac{4}{4}$ meter.

Example 4-15 shows parallel passages from the first-movement exposition and recapitulation of Mozart's *String Quartet*, K. 421. Although the passages are disposed differently in rela-

4–15. Mozart, *String Quartet*, K. 421, first movement

4–15. *(Continued)*

tion to the notated first and third beats, they are the same in metric structure. Several passages in this movement group half-note pulses by odd numbers, causing such shifts. One such passage is illustrated in example 4-16. Metric shifts of this type are common in all tonal styles and are discussed more extensively later in this chapter under the subheading "Meter and Metric Notation."

Possible changes in grouping more than one level above the primary metric level affect phrase rhythm—a subject discussed in chapters 6, 7, and 9.

Metric Changes Where the Notated Measure Is a Single Pulse. Although tonal composers before the later part of the nineteenth century rarely notated changes of grouping at the primary metric level, they did have a way of including such changes. If the notated

4–16. Mozart, *String Quartet*, K. 421, first movement

measure is the pulse at the primary level, changes in grouping can be effected merely by changing the number of measures in a group. This occurs frequently in scherzos and other fast movements. Review example 3-36 for such a change in the first movement of Beethoven's *Fifth*. Occasionally, the composer indicated the number of measures in a group by means of words, such as *"Ritmo di tre battute"* and *"Ritmo di quattro battute"* in the scherzo of Beethoven's *Ninth Symphony*, and *"Si ha s'immaginar la battuta di* $\frac{6}{8}$*"* in the trio of his *String Quartet*, op. 74. It may be that Beethoven annotated these passages because the indicated groupings continue for long passages. For in many other movements, groupings change frequently.

It is probable that composers used measures as pulses in order to gain the flexibility of changing meters in scherzos and other fast movements. But what they lost in the process is the possibility of showing the location of the downbeats. Even when they used the annotations just described to specify the number of measures in a group, they did not locate the measures functioning as downbeats. And where such annotations are not used, varying interpretations of grouping as well as of the location of downbeats are equally plausible. The scherzo to Beethoven's *Seventh Symphony* is a case in point (example 4-17). The very opening establishes the notated measures as groupings of quarter notes by durational accents in the bass, contour accents in the melody, and then by the bass notes causing textural accents at the beginning of each measure. The durational accents in the melody, beginning in measure 6, confirm the measure units. The tempo ensures that the measure is a pulse at the primary metric level.

It seems from the very opening bars that measures are grouped in pairs. There are two measures of forte, the second a sequence of

4–17. Beethoven, *Symphony No. 7*, op. 92, third movement

4–17. (Continued)

the first. Then the piano appears. If this hypothesis is adopted by the listener, one can continue grouping the measures in pairs, with each odd-numbered measure receiving an accent. In support of this hypothesis are the change in texture at measure 11, the first of the sforzandos in measure 15, and the forte in measure 17 (reinforced in measure 17 and again in measure 19 by a durational accent in the melody). Since this section contains an even number of measures (24), the pairing of measures can continue on the repeat.

If measures are paired throughout this section, however, several factors contradict this grouping. The changes in harmony in measures 6 and 10, supported by durational accents in the melody, occur on even-numbered measures. And although the measure-by-measure alternation of V and I in A major (measures 17–22) can be perceived strong-weak just as well as weak-strong, the two-measure A-major arpeggio in measures 22–23 is hard to imagine as weak-strong. And if measure 22 is strong, no continuous pairing of measures is possible through the repeat sign.

A flexible approach to groupings here might pair measures 1–2, then begin the theme in measure 3 with a strong measure set off

4–17. *(Continued)*

by the change in dynamics, theme, and texture. If a three-measure group is perceived in measures 3–5, the change of harmony in measure 6 sets off duple groups of measures for the remainder of the section until measure 21. According to this interpretation, the durational accents in measures 6, 10, 12, and 14 in the melody and 18 and 20 in the bass are on strong measures—the factors enumerated in support of our first hypothesis are now the counteraccents. The last three measures (22–24) might be perceived as a three-grouping leading back to the opening pair. Or 22–24 might retain the strong-weak-strong status, forcing a reinterpretation of measures 1–2 on the repeat.

No definitive version is possible among these conflicting accent-causing factors. The music following the double bar at first seems to opt for one version, but then contradicts this in such a way that one's confidence in these groupings ends up rather shaken. See measures 25–73 in example 4-18.

At first, four-measure groupings are set off by changes in pattern, texture, harmony, and dynamics. This pattern is so strong that the sudden fortissimo in measures 43–44 and 59–60 can be perceived as articulating the fourth measures of some of these groupings. This interpretation favors the first of our alternatives to measure 1–24 for the theme in measures 11–14. But when the opening material enters in B♭, beginning in measure 64, it would be on a weak measure if the preceding four-groupings have been maintained. The same situation leads to the return of the opening in F in measure 89. Because these two returns to the opening are an odd number of measures apart (25), some change in groupings must occur if the two returns are to have the same metric status.

In sum, whatever the approach, groupings of beats will change. The contradictory accentuation patterns are part of the rhythm of the piece. That they cannot be reconciled into a single version can lead to two attitudes on the part of the listener or performer. A listener or performer might try to impose one pattern, perhaps recognizing that this is only one of several possibilities. Or he or she might try to remain neutral about these accentuations—allowing the interplay of the conflicting accentuations to project as the rhythm and meter of the passage.

Hemiola. In triple meter, one particular type of metric change, known as *hemiola,* is very common. Hemiola is a change from a 3 + 3 grouping of six beats to a 2 + 2 + 2 grouping. In other words, hemiola is a change from $^6_4$ to $^3_2$. Hemiolas often occur just before a cadence, as in the excerpts in example 4-19. In the Mozart excerpt, the textural accents and harmonic changes, along with the patterning in the right hand, make it clear that measures 8–9 are in $^3_2$. It is hard to imagine a manner of hearing the downbeat of measure 9 as a downbeat, even on first acquaintance with the passage. In the two other excerpts, however, the factors creating the hemiola are not the only accent producers present. In the Bach excerpt, there is a chord change on the downbeat to the penultimate measure, even though the upper two voices are tied across the barline. In the Brahms excerpt, there may be no attack at all on the downbeat of measure 43. But there is only a single moving part in measures 42–

4–18. Beethoven, *Symphony No. 7*, op. 92, third movement

4–18. (Continued)

114

4–18. *(Continued)*

Mozart, *Piano Sonata*, K. 283, first movement

Bach, *English Suite No. 3*, first movement

4–19

Brahms, *Symphony No. 2*, op. 73, first movement

4–19. *(Continued)*

43 within a sustained harmony. The decision whether to hear hemiola or syncopation within $\frac{3}{4}$ in the Bach and Brahms excerpts may
well rest with the listener.

Part of the reason that hemiola often allows for such alternative modes of hearing is that the six beats involved in the hemiola fill
two notated measures. Unlike metric change in excerpts such as the
scherzo to Beethoven's *Seventh* discussed above, in which metric
changes force a reinterpretation of the entire metric hierarchy,

hemiola—regardless of how it is organized by the listener—will not disrupt the regularity of alternate downbeats.

METER AND METRIC NOTATION

Several examples have demonstrated that meter signatures and metric notations are not necessarily accurate in denoting the primary metric level in all tonal pieces or passages. A range of factors can cause a discrepancy between the notated meter and the structural metric hierarchy. Some of these factors have been mentioned already and need but little amplification here. Others have not yet been discussed.

In tonal compositions where the grouping of pulses on the primary level changes during the course of a movement, tonal composers before the late nineteenth century usually notated the pulse as a full measure and did not indicate the groupings at all. They apparently preferred this method of notation to the inclusion of changing meter signatures. We have already witnessed this in the first movement of Beethoven's *Fifth Symphony* (example 3-36) and in the scherzo of Beethoven's *Seventh Symphony* (examples 4-17 and 4-18).

Passages in which the notated measure is a pulse may arise in a movement in which the primary metric level has changed from one passage to another. The body of Tchaikovsky's *Romeo and Juliet Fantasy-Overture,* for instance, is notated in C throughout (allegro giusto, measures 111–483). At the opening of the allegro giusto, the quarter note is clearly the pulse on the primary metric level. Quarters, syncopated quarters, eighths, and sixteenths are the predominant durations. Harmonic changes occur at least once a measure, and occasionally even on every eighth note. In the transition to the second theme group (measures 160–82), the level of activity in several areas slows down dramatically. Harmonic changes occur every few measures only, and eventually do not occur for eight measures. Sixteenths and eighths become more infrequent and eventually drop out, as do even quarter notes, leaving half notes as the shortest values in measures 179–82. Even though the metronomic tempo has not changed, the primary metric level of the love theme (beginning in measure 183) is at the half-note or even the whole-note level. The harmonies change every one or two measures now, and quarter notes are the fastest values. The C meter signature may indicate both the pulse and its grouping at the beginning of the allegro giusto. But it does not do the same in the love theme.

In this Tchaikovsky piece, the primary metric level changes between two passages while the metric notation remains the same. In other pieces more than one plausible metric level is apparent in the music of a single passage. In Bach's $A\flat$-*Major Prelude* (review example 3-24), a primary pulse is plausible at more than one level.

Barlines misplaced by half a measure are common in pieces written in a compound duple meter, such as $\frac{4}{4}$, $\frac{12}{8}$, or even $\frac{6}{8}$. We have already encountered one such composition in Mozart's *String Quartet*, K. 421 (example 4-15).

In the case of metric ambiguity or change, the notated meter may reflect only one of the possible choices, and not necessarily the most compelling one. In addition to the excerpts cited earlier in the section on metric ambiguity, consider the second theme in the finale of Schumann's *Piano Concerto* in example 4-20. Taken in isolation, the passage beginning at measure 190 seems to be in $\frac{3}{2}$. Except for the fact that the listener continues the notated $\frac{3}{4}$ meter, there is no factor that supports $\frac{3}{4}$. Cooper and Meyer note the strong duple grouping of quarters, but assert that a latent $\frac{3}{4}$ meter "continues in the minds and motor responses of the audience as well as of the performer, making the music seem somewhat strained."[8] But can we assume such an automatic retention of the previous meter here? A $\frac{3}{4}$ meter in this passage can only be supported by a willful effort on the part of the listener—an effort that is quite difficult to sustain for long with such a lack of supporting features. It is difficult to imagine how a performer might project $\frac{3}{4}$ here.

This is only one of many examples in which Schumann's meter signatures do not agree with the metric structure. Although the metric notation in example 4-20 can be defended because of its placement in the middle of a movement, occasional other pieces of his seem to be notated with an almost purposeful perversity. One such movement is the scherzo of the *Piano Quintet*, op. 44. Example 4-21 presents the opening and second trio. Here, as throughout the scherzo, the functional barline is the middle of each measure. In these two Schumann excerpts, the metric notation may have an intended psychological effect on the performer. Even though it may not be possible for the performer to project this meter or for the audience to perceive it, the metric conflict may be a factor in that intangible essence of a dramatic performance.

4–20. Schumann, *Piano Concerto,* third movement

Finally, metric notations are sometimes dictated by conventions of a given era. In late eighteenth-century music, for instance, many fast movements in $\frac{3}{8}$ feature groupings of measures in twos or even fours throughout. In the finale of Mozart's *Violin Concerto No. 3,* K. 216, $\frac{3}{8}$ measures are grouped in fours for almost the entirety of the $\frac{3}{8}$ sections. (The middle section of the movement is notated in **C**.) If the movement were notated in $\frac{12}{8}$, the larger metric structure would be self-evident. Only one passage (measures 159–210) would have to shift the functional downbeat to the middle of the measure—a change that, as we have already seen, is common in

119

4–21. Schumann, *Piano Quintet,* op. 44, third movement

music notated in $\frac{12}{8}$. (The fermatas in measures 217, 251, and 377 also disrupt the four-groupings. But the fermatas may have been Mozart's preference over several measures of rest or sustained notes.)

On the surface, it seems that the only difference between $\frac{4}{4}$ and $\frac{12}{8}$ is the subdivision of the beats. We would never expect to see a $\frac{4}{4}$-type movement notated in $\frac{1}{4}$ with measures grouped in fours. So

4–21. *(Continued)*

why should Mozart have used $\frac{3}{8}$ and not $\frac{12}{8}$? The answer lies in notational conventions. $\frac{12}{8}$ is a meter signature associated predominantly with slow movements.

Matters of tempo also control the selection of the notated unit
of pulse at the primary metric level. Slower movements tend to use
shorter values as the pulse (quarters, eighths, and even
sixteenths)—thereby emphasizing the slow tempo by notating a

4–21. (Continued)

short value at a slow pace. Fast movements by contrast tend to use longer values as pulses (quarters, halves, dotted halves, even whole notes), emphasizing the speed by having longer values go by so fast. This affects the options for a meter signature. In a very fast movement with a long value as the pulse, there may be few ways to avoid that each pulse has to be notated as a measure. The finale of Beethoven's *Eighth Symphony,* for instance, is in ¢, *allegro vivace* (o = 84). The haste of the whole notes and the almost impossible speed of the faster values (even assuming that Beethoven's metronome markings must be taken as too fast) help communicate the extreme haste of this movement to the performer. After he decided to use the whole note as the beat, what measure length other than the whole note could Beethoven have used? Even though for much of the movement measures are in pairs, a meter signature of $\frac{4}{2}$ or $\frac{2}{1}$ might have suggested the stately movement of an archaic, religious compositional mode.

NOTATED METER AND METRIC ANALYSIS

Since factors other than the metric structure can influence a composer's choice of a meter signature, an analyst should abstain from resorting to the metric notation to assert one metric structure over another in an ambiguous passage. Listeners may hear the harmonic rhythm, the durational accents, textural accents, patterns of repetition, the context, and other factors that can create a meter. But without a score, they cannot hear the metric notation. If the musical structure cannot project a meter to the listener, the notation cannot do so either.

The fifth of Bach's *Twelve Little Preludes* provides a case in point. Both Cooper and Meyer as well as Yeston comment on the meter here. Cooper and Meyer note that "without the time signature, $\frac{3}{4}$, the grouping might have been interpreted as being $2 \times \frac{3}{8}$, instead of $3 \times \frac{2}{8}$. . . . But, in view of meter signature, it would be wrong."[9] For Yeston, meter arises from the interaction of two strata of motion. Yeston's approach to meter requires that one choose among possible middlegrounds to group a foreground by evaluating each for the greatest interest. This Bach prelude is the subject of his first metric analysis. He notes the two potential groupings of eighths. "At this point the most important question to

4–22. Bach, *Prelude in D* (No. 5 of Twelve Little Preludes), BWV926

Bach / Twelve Little Preludes, no. 5

4–23. Maury Yeston, *The Stratification of Musical Rhythm*, example 3.8

be asked involves the alternate grouping of level B. Why is this not a valid accentual interpretation. . . .? If the compositional intent is an essentially static *d,* with triadic embellishments, then a $\frac{6}{8}$ meter is called for and the reading of level B is relevant. But if the essential musical motion is intended as a purposeful sweep from root to third to fifth of the tonic triad, then the $\frac{3}{4}$ time signature is more appropriate."[10] Although Yeston proceeds to note that "the time signature represents nothing more than a graphic technology that helps to indicate which particular middleground structure is meant to shape the foreground" (that is, how the pulses are organized), he essentially argues for the meter signature as the decisive factor here. For how else except through the meter signature can he possibly know what Bach's "compositional intent" was—whether it was the "purposeful sweep from root to third" or the "essentially static *d*"?

In fact, there is little evidence here to argue decisively in favor of $\frac{6}{8}$ or $\frac{3}{4}$. Once a listener has settled on either option, he or she can easily maintain that structure during the opening of the piece. Not until measure 10 (see example 4-24) is there a confirmation of one of the two meters—the notated $\frac{3}{4}$. When the opening motive returns in measure 11 in the now confirmed $\frac{3}{4}$ meter, the listener gets to learn this organization of the motive. As we have argued earlier in this chapter in connection with other metrically ambiguous passages, the listener's memory of this structuring of the motive when he or she returns to the opening is the decisive factor in hearing the notated meter right from measure 1. If the listener assumes $\frac{6}{8}$ on first hearing, he or she cannot possibly be aware of the greater interest of the $\frac{3}{4}$ rendering (compare the comments concerning the sarabande rhythm of example 4-2). The listener cannot know the meter signature or Bach's intent. But he or she can and most certainly will hear the patterning of measures 10, 14, 15, 17, 20–25, and so forth.

Charles Smith, in his thorough critique of Yeston's study,[11]

4–24. Bach, *Prelude in D* (No. 5 of Twelve Little Preludes), BWV 926

124

criticizes Yeston for weighing only the $\frac{6}{8}$ and $\frac{3}{4}$ alternatives as possible groupings of the right-hand eighths. Smith illustrates a host of other possible groupings: in sixes with one or more notes as upbeats, in sevens, and so forth. These possibilities might reside in the right-hand part but are hardly plausible as metric groupings because of the left-hand notes on every downbeat.

One might regard this keyboard prelude as too simple and too étude-like a piece to spend so much effort on. Surely Bach's reputation would not long survive if this passage were our only extant relic of his output. But the issues raised here affect other, more substantive pieces. Consider the opening of the finale of his *Sonata in G Minor for Violin Alone* (example 4-25).[12]

4-25. Bach, *Sonata No. 1 for Violin Alone*, BWV 1001, fourth movement

At the very opening, $\frac{3}{16}$ groupings seem to be the most easily perceptible. And, according to Yeston's criterion of greater interest, the $\frac{3}{16}$ grouping, with two chord notes on beats in each measure, seems preferable to the alternative $\frac{3}{8}$ grouping with one chord note per measure (see example 4-26). After all, the arpeggio in measure 4 ascends through each note of the chord, seemingly supporting the

4-26

$\frac{3}{16}$ groupings. But here the apparent interest of the $\frac{3}{16}$ pales in relation to the long-range interest of the $\frac{3}{8}$ grouping. For the notes emphasized by the $\frac{3}{8}$ grouping give rise to the four-voiced G-minor triad in example 4-27. This voicing opens and closes the first-movement adagio (as well as framing the first phrase within that movement), closes the second-movement fugue, and closes this finale. The arpeggiation in measures 4 and 5 of the finale contains these notes one at a time on each beat. In any event, even if a listener begins by hearing the piece in $\frac{3}{16}$, he or she will have to change to $\frac{3}{8}$ during the later passages, which clearly group sixteenths in pairs.

4–27

5

MULTIPLE METRIC LEVELS
AND STYLE

The way in which the various levels of a metric hierarchy interact with one another relates closely to what we call musical style. This chapter explores such metric interactions within the context of two major style changes in the history of tonal music—the contrasting profiles of Baroque versus Classic-Romantic metric hierarchies, and a new type of interaction that arose in the late nineteenth century and that contributed to the dissolution of tonality.

The exploration here builds upon the discussion at the end of chapter 3 concerning the varied metric profiles of Bach's *Prelude in Ab Major* (*Well-Tempered Clavier*, II), Mozart's *Symphony No. 40*, and Beethoven's *Symphony No. 5*. That discussion noted both similarities and differences between these passages. All three excerpts feature complete or nearly complete metric hierarchies. And in all three passages, the harmonic changes occur at first at a multi-measure pacing (every two measures in the Bach and Mozart works, every four measures in the Beethoven symphony).

But there is a crucial difference that sets the Mozart and Beethoven excerpts apart from the Bach prelude. In the Mozart and Beethoven openings, the regularity of patternings and accentuations at the fastest levels causes these faster levels to function primarily as subdivisions of the larger groupings. In the Bach passage, on the other hand, the greater complexity of accentuation patterns at the fastest levels causes these fastest levels to become a possible focus of attention. As noted in chapter 3, the tempo taken in this Bach prelude largely determines whether the eighth-to-sixteenth-to-thirty-second levels or the quarter-to-measure-to-two-measure levels receive the sharpest focus. Such a choice of focal points is possible in this piece because of interesting and complex features at

127

many levels in the metric hierarchy. No listener would follow the eighths of the viola part at the opening of Mozart's *Fortieth* or in the melody at the beginning of Beethoven's *Fifth* the way he or she might follow the sixteenths and thirty-seconds throughout Bach's prelude. Hence, no listener would wish for a performance of these Mozart and Beethoven works at a tempo so slow that the eighth notes were brought into focus but the two-measure or four-measure units were so long that they would lose their unity.

The multileveled structuring of important activity occurring in Bach's *Ab Major Prelude* characterizes much of his music, an aspect of his style to which some recent writers on rhythm have called attention. Edward Cone notes the primacy of the beat in Bach's music and the interaction of various types of patternings of fast note values that creates the vitality of Bach's motor rhythms.[1] Robert Cogan and Pozzi Escot describe how various pacings of activity arise against a continuous motor rhythm in the *Allemande* of Bach's *French Suite No. 4*.[2] But multiple levels of essential activity affect not only the patterning in Bach's motor-rhythm passages but pervade many aspects of his style, such as the nature of harmonic motions, textures, and counterpoint. The following section and later portions of this chapter take note of these aspects in some characteristic excerpts.

MULTIPLE LEVELS OF ACTIVITY IN SOME BACH WORKS

Fugue in C Minor (Well-Tempered Clavier, I). Multiple levels of activity in the *Fugue in C Minor* proceed from several characteristics of Bach's style. The implied polyphony in single voice parts and the resulting arpeggiations and voice leadings among several strands within each voice part create continuous, multiply accented pulses at the fastest metric levels. A slower melodic pacing arises within each melodic strand. A harmonic sense derived from figured-bass generates rapid harmonic changes over the bass part, along with a slower pacing of more essential harmonies.

The two-tiered voice leading within the subject gives rise to two levels of activity right from the beginning. (See example 5-1.) There is the note-to-note activity in eighths and sixteenths. And there is the half-note pacing of events in the lower strand—a strand that functions as bass to the upper one. The interaction of the two strands is emphasized by the fact that the lower one is an augmented

5–1. Bach, *Fugue in C Minor (Well-Tempered Clavier, I)*

inversion of the recurring fragment in the upper one (C-B-C-D; G-A♭-G-F).

Just as melodic activity occurs at the two separate pacings noted in example 5-1, harmonic activity reinforces these two levels of activity throughout most of the fugue. Consider the initial bass entry of the subject in measures 7–9 in example 5-2. This is the first appearance in the fugue of a three-voiced texture—a texture that then persists until the end. Plausible harmonic motions occur both on the eighth-note-sixteenth-note and the half-note levels. In the more rapid stratum, the VII₆ chord that ends measure 6 resolves to I on the downbeat of measure 7. The C-B-C sixteenths in the bass during the first half of measure 7 support E♭-D-C in the soprano, implying a I-V₆-I prolongation of this tonic. The bass G on the fourth eighth of the measure supports the A♭-G to imply a dominant that resolves deceptively to IV₆ on beat 3. By the last eighth of the measure, this IV₆ has become a II before arriving on the cadential ⁶₄ on the downbeat of measure 8. The progression from IV₆ to II within measure 7 is itself prolonged by a neighboring tonic on beat 4, itself preceded by VII₇. Plausible harmonic motion on this level continues throughout the subject statement.

5–2. Bach, *Fugue in C Minor (Well-Tempered Clavier, I)*

The same voice leading that produces these rapid harmonic changes also presents harmonic motion on the half-note level. (See example 5-3.) The end of measure 6, heard as a half-note harmony, is a II_7 chord. There is no bass on the downbeat of measure 7. The members of a I chord following the II_7 do not allow a resolution of the II_7. So when the bass G appears on the fourth eighth of the measure, it functions as bass for the preceding half measure, forming a cadential $^6_4$ (review the outline of the subject in example 5-1). The soprano sixteenths during the first half of measure 7 fill in E♭-G, while the beginning of the subject presents C. The second half of measure 7 is IV_6-becoming-II^4_3, functioning as a neighboring harmony between the cadential $^6_4$'s on the first halves of measures 7 and 8.

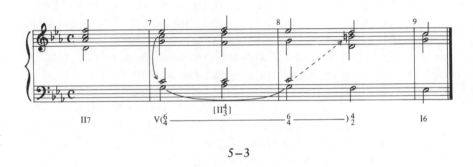

5–3

To be sure, most tonal pieces have harmonic motions on larger levels elaborated or prolonged by more surface harmonies. What distinguishes this and other Bach passages from the music of later periods is that harmonic-melodic interaction causes functionally meaningful harmonic motion at the very fastest metric levels in the piece on a continuous basis. In Mozart's *Fortieth,* Beethoven's *Fifth,* Brahms' *First,* or any of the other excerpts that we discussed in earlier chapters, activity at the fastest metric levels involves elaboration of longer harmonies and not plausible harmonic activity in its own right.[3]

Indeed, the double level of harmonic motion in many Bach works is part of what makes these works so appealing to an amateur keyboard player. In a fast Beethoven, Brahms, Schumann, or Liszt piece, struggling to hit all the sixteenths easily results in a tempo too slow to allow the larger melodic-harmonic motions to make any sense at all. In a Bach piece, the fastest level of activity often makes some sense, even when taken more slowly than a well-considered performance would attempt.

Cantata No. 140 (Wachet auf, ruft uns die Stimme), Opening Chorus. The contrapuntal texture of the *Fugue in C Minor* features similar levels of activity in each voice part. Another type of contrapuntal texture in Bach's works features melodic voice parts (not pedals or sustained accompanimental parts) moving at dramatically different rates. In such textures, the different rates of speed of the melodic voices create the multileveled structure. Often the slowest part in such textures is a chorale or another preexistent melody treated as a cantus firmus. Among the numerous such settings that include a slow chorale melody in a faster texture is the opening chorus of *Cantata No. 140* (example 5-4).

Several levels of activity are present even during the opening ritornello. The one-measure changes in harmony complement the timbral antiphony (upper strings versus double-reeds) to establish a measure-long unit contrasting with the dotted-eighth sixteenth and sixteenth-note figurations. This movement does not exhibit much of the fast harmonic rhythm level that characterizes the *Fugue in C Minor*. Instead, it features a contrast of levels of motivic activity.

During the phrase-by-phrase presentation of the chorale melody, a slower pacing joins this texture, but without interfering with the faster levels. The first chorale phrase, for instance, by itself outlines the E♭ tonic triad with a single neighbor motion of B♭-C-B♭. The stability of this eight-note phrase presented over ten measures encompasses the measure-long harmonies and antiphonal timbre changes, as well as the faster rhythms above and below the melody.

As some of the textural components continue through the cadences and caesuras in other components, the independence of each is emphasized. The first chorale phrase, for instance, arrives on its final note on the downbeat of measure 25. This downbeat also marks the harmonic arrival on B♭ and the beginning of a new statement of the opening of the ritornello. But the imitative chorus parts extend past the downbeat. And the first-violin sixteenths ignore the cadence entirely, not coming to a rest until the downbeat of measure 26, where the strings join in the antiphony of the ritornello already underway—all this while the last chorale note still resonates.

5–4. Bach, *Cantata No. 140,* first movement

5–4. *(Continued)*

5–4. *(Continued)*

5–4. (*Continued*)

5–4. (Continued)

5–4. (*Continued*)

MULTILEVELED STRUCTURES IN BAROQUE VERSUS LATER MUSIC

Textures containing continuous motor rhythms or the multileveled melodic pacings of Bach do occur in later music, but rarely if ever with the effect of creating the multitiered structures so characteristic of Bach's music. Either the motor rhythm projects a repetitious patterning in an accompaniment, at a pace far removed from the essential harmonic and phrasing activity (as in Mozart's *Symphony No. 40*, as well as in pieces such as Chopin's *Prelude in G Major*, op. 28, no. 3), or the motor rhythm is the leading melody, similarly removed in metric level from essential activity in harmony and phrasing, and with the intermediate metric levels only weakly articulated (as at the opening of Beethoven's *Fifth*, in perpetual motions, or in textures such as the opening of the finale in Mendelssohn's *Violin Concerto*).

Nowhere is the contrast between Bachian and later motor-rhythm textures more vividly illustrated than in the accompaniments added by Bach and Robert Schumann to the *preludio* from Bach's *E Major Partita for Violin Alone* (BWV 1006). The *preludio* features continuous unaccompanied sixteenths almost throughout. Bach's setting is the sinfonia to *Cantata No. 29*, with the violin solo part assigned to the organ obbligato. Robert Schumann composed a piano accompaniment to the movement as part of his settings of all six Bach sonatas and partitas for violin alone.

Bach's setting emphasizes the articulation of several levels in the metric hierarchy with continuous eighths and with other factors articulating quarters and measures in most passages. Schumann's accompaniment features fewer factors articulating metric levels below the notated measure. Where his setting introduces syncopations in the accompaniment, it does so within the *"Schwung"* of the measure. Example 5-5 illustrates parallel passages from both settings. The setting in *Cantata No. 29* is in D major, in line with Bach's customary practice of transposing down a whole step when transcribing a solo part from strings to keyboard.[4]

What is perhaps most striking about these two arrangements is the obvious circumstance that the melody is identical in both and that the harmonies are mostly the same. The different stylistic worlds that the two versions inhabit is the result of neither melody nor harmony (including harmonic rhythm). The few differences in chord choice between Schumann and Bach are relatively minor details. It is largely texture and its resulting accentuations and articulations of various metric levels that determine the differences. Schumann interpreted Bach's melody according to his own aesthetic rather than Bach's.

Schumann was not alone in his reinterpretations of Bach's works. Probably the most famous nineteenth-century transformation of a Bach work is Gounod's *Ave Maria* that uses the *Prelude in C Major* (*Well Tempered Clavier, I*) as its accompaniment. Edward

5–5. Bach, *Cantata No. 29*, sinfonia

5–5. *(Continued)*

Cone has discussed the multiple patternings that enliven Bach's prelude[5] (see example 5-6). But for Gounod, the arpeggiations were not a finely etched surface, but an accompaniment figuration. Indeed, when we listen to Gounod's setting, with its broad phrases spanning four or more measures, the intricacies of the sixteenth-note patterns cease to be the object of attention. Bach's layered structures, as in the opening chorus of *Cantata No. 140* (review ex-

5–5. *(Continued)*

ample 5-4), maintain the integrity of the separate levels by articulating vividly all the levels in the metric hierarchy. In Gounod's *Ave Maria,* the sixteenth-note and eighth-note patternings are too far removed from the four-measure level and exhibit insufficient intermediate articulation for both to be simultaneous focuses of attention. If anything, it is precisely because the *C Major Prelude* is a Baroque foreground that it is somewhat less than satisfactory as an

5–5. *(Continued)*

accompanimental patterning. It does not act as a good nineteenth-century accompaniment should—at the melodic climaxes the melody cries out for the sixteenths to break out of their patterning and expand in register, become tremolos, or do the sorts of things that nineteenth-century accompaniments do.

The other type of texture in Bach's music that gives rise to es-

Schumann, *Piano Accompaniment to Bach's Partita No. 3*

5–5. (Continued)

5–6

sential activity on divergent levels of the metric hierarchy involves the presence of a cantus firmus. The cantus firmus is either a chorale (as in *Wachet auf*) or a melody or transformation of a melody stated earlier in that composition. The stately opening subject of the *St. Ann's Fugue* (BWV 552) recurs several times as a slow cantus firmus during the third section of the fugue—a section that features another subject moving at a much faster pace. A similar, though not quite so contrasting combination of pacings arises in triple fugues (see measures 94ff., *passim*, in the *Fugue in C♯ Minor, Well-Tempered Clavier*, I), or in fugues when an augmentation of the subject appears (as in measures 14–16, *passim*, in the *Fugue in C Minor, Well-Tempered Clavier*, II).

Such textures are, by and large, anomalies in the music of the later-eighteenth and nineteenth centuries. And when they do occur, they do not create the effect of essential motion on two levels that the comparable textures in Bach's music create. Consider the concluding pages of Wagner's *Walküre*. As Brünnhilde falls asleep, Wotan summons Loge to ignite his magical fire as protection for the sleeping Valkyrie. The "magic fire" music, in a moderate tempo, features continuous sixteenth-note activity, and local harmony changes in half notes, quarter notes, and occasionally even in eighths, with some neighboring harmonies in sixteenths. New harmonic areas and other changes mark off phrases every few measures. As Wotan then decrees that no one who fears his spear shall ever cross the ring of fire, the majestic introduction of the Siegfried leitmotif allows us a glimpse of his thoughts. Siegfried's leitmotif enters as a cantus firmus, eight measures for each phrase subdivision. And since, in Wagner's characteristic construction, the phrase subdivisions—eight measures each—begin as sequences, the new theme moves considerably slower than the preceding and surrounding fire music.

But the effect is not that of Bach's chorale-prelude textures. In the opening chorus of *Wachet auf,* the faster music proceeds at its own pace during the appearances of the cantus firmus. In *Die Walküre,* the fire music becomes an accompaniment to Siegfried's leitmotif, following the harmonic implications of the slower theme. In essence, the result is similar to rhythmically activated accompaniments in late-eighteenth and other nineteenth-century music. See, for instance, the slow movement of Schubert's *Quintet in C,* op. 163 (especially the third section of the movement), where there is quite a bit of surface activity against the slow chorale-textured theme. Yet all the surface activity is filigree—stellar filigree, but filigree nonetheless, supporting the essential pacing of the chorale texture that lies at the heart of the movement. Perhaps the change in pacing and the submersion of the faster activity that takes place in *Die Walküre* upon the cantus-firmus entrance of Siegfried's leitmotif is most obvious after the conclusion of the cantus firmus. Where the magic fire music is generally active at and below the measure level before the cantus firmus appears, it merely marks off multiply repeated measures after the cantus firmus. The faster level of activity has been absorbed by the cantus firmus.

NESTED VERSUS UNSYNCHRONIZED LEVELS

In the overwhelming majority of the tonal repertoire, durational patterns at any given level of the metric hierarchy subdivide the longer patterns at the next higher level of the hierarchy. Sixteenths in pairs subdivide eighths, eighths in pairs subdivide quarters, and so forth. In this relationship, subdivisions may be said to nest within one another.

Virtually all the metric structures discussed in this book so far are nested structures. Exceptions are mostly in those passages where the grouping at a given level does not nest within the next higher level but does synchronize with durational patterns two and more levels higher. One such situation occurs when triplet-eighths appear in a passage that hitherto features pairs of eighths subdividing quarters. The triplets are shorter than the eighths, but do not group to form eighths. At the next higher level, both pairs of eighths and groups of three triplets agree in forming quarters. In other terminology, the triplet and eighth beat divisions are unsynchronized, but both nest within quarters. The same relationships arise in triple

145

meter when hemiola is present. There is a lack of synchronization between pairs of beats and the measure unit, but both the hemiola and the three-beat measures nest within two-measure groups.

Although patternings that are potentially metric do not often occur in the tonal repertoire out of synchronization with any higher level, instances of this do arise, mostly in music of the late nineteenth century. Listen to the excerpt in example 5-7 for one instance. The left-hand sixteenths group in threes on the basis of patterning and implied harmonic changes. The beginnings of these three-groupings coordinate with every fourth eighth. But since the patterning begins on the second sixteenth of the notated measures, the coordination between eighths and groupings of three sixteenths never occurs on notated downbeats. Only one of these two possible coordinations between three-sixteenth groupings and the right-hand eighths occurs in each measure, since the patterning breaks off each time after three groupings.

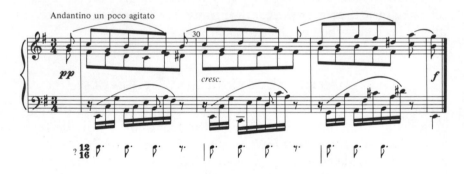

5–7. Brahms, *Intermezzo*, op. 119, no. 2

Earlier in this intermezzo, the quarter-note pulse undergoes changes in grouping (hemiola) and subdivision (eighths and sixteenths versus triplets). But the integrity of the quarter note as pulse remains intact. As a result, the unsynchronized three-sixteenth groupings in measures 29–31 are probably perceived by most listeners as cross-accentuations against the quarter-note pulse. The resulting interpretations of the points of harmonic change as anticipations or delays from the quarter-note pulses are in line with such adjustments mandated by other factors during much of the piece. See the opening measures in example 5-8, in which a pure tonic

5–8. Brahms, *Intermezzo,* op. 119, no. 2

never appears because of conchordal neighbors whenever the left hand presents the tonic.

Unsynchronized passages occur on a larger scale in music by other composers in the 1890s and later. The last portions of the first-movement development section from Mahler's *Third Symphony* (composed in 1896) provide some cases in point. In this, as in many other of his works, Mahler often builds a section out of several short, easily identifiable motives, which are then assembled and reassembled in different ways. Beginning at study number 2 (measure 27), for instance, four separate elements appear (see example 5-9). Following this, and continuing until after study number 4 (measure 49), these four elements are juxtaposed in ever-changing ways, some of which are illustrated in example 5-10.

Juxtaposition of separate elements also occurs on a large scale at this movement, especially in the development section. Beginning at study number 49, for instance, two or three separate levels of ac-

[Kräftig. Entschieden] Schwer und dumpf.

5–9. Mahler, *Symphony No. 3,* first movement

5–10. Mahler, *Symphony No. 3,* first movement

tivity run against one another (see example 5-11). Although each level is in the notated $\frac{4}{4}$ meter, the disparity of their pacings is so great that they almost sound like two pieces occurring simultaneously. The phrasing of the brass melody is in two-measure units (2 + 2 and 2 + 2) with no cadence before measure 8, while the woodwind fanfare is phrased in one-measure subdivisions (1 + 1 + 2; then 2 + 2 with a second voice entering on the second measure and joining the already present melody in the next measure).

The strands are also separate from each other harmonically. The fourth measure is subdominant in the brass and tonic in the winds. The disparities between the implied or stated harmonies in the brass and winds is greater in the next four measures. Mean-

5–11. Mahler, *Symphony No. 3,* first movement

while, the bass moves slower still, implying a dominant to tonic over the eight measures, although with B♭, not B♮ in measure 7.

Simultaneous music with disparate levels of activity continues for most of the remainder of the development. The disparity of pacings is heightened at the very end of the section by actual changes in the tempo of the different strands. Two measures before study number 53, for instance, the fanfare in the E♭ clarinet carries a notated accelerando during the steady beat in the simultaneously sounding parts. And at the very end of the section, the snare drums enter in a new tempo "without any regard to the cellos and basses"[6] (the only other instruments playing at the time). The cello and bass parts carry their own annotation, reminding them to "continue in the tempo without regard to the snare drums, which begin in the opening march-tempo."[7] The separation of percussion and lower strings here is heightened by the physical distance separating the orchestra proper from the drums placed at a distance.

Such wide divergencies in pacing, found in many Mahler works, were a powerful influence on Schoenberg and his colleagues. One of the factors promoting the relaxation of tonal functions in Schoenberg's transitional works between tonality and atonality is the increasingly serendipitous nature of the harmonies that arise in polyphonic textures, especially where different themes are juxtaposed, each with its own pacing.

In the *Chamber Symphony,* op. 9 (composed in 1906), for instance, the initial statements of themes are most often supported by harmonies and harmonic progressions with at least vestiges of functional tonal meaning. At the very opening of the piece, for instance, the fourth-chord slides into an altered dominant seventh with both a raised and lowered fifth before the latter chord resolves to an F-major triad. To be sure, the resulting simultaneities, when viewed as pitch-class sets, provide the essential structures for much of the piece (the diatonic versus whole-tone scalar resources, and the symmetrical versus nonsymmetrical tonal structures). But there is at least a vestige of pre-dominant to dominant to tonic. The same harmonic structures, this time heading toward E (with F now heard as Neapolitan), prepare and support the opening themes of the *Sehr rasch* that follows the introduction (see example 5-12). Similar types of harmonic interaction arise at the introduction of most themes in this four-movements-in-one composition.

But during other sections of the piece, including transitional and developmental passages, the interactions that occur do not retain even these tonal hints. A rather complex but not unrepresentative passage occurs after a pause in the middle of the development section (see example 5-13). The effect of varied pacings, phrase lengths, and harmonic implications of each part has no parallel in tonal music of earlier periods.

It may in part have been the multileveled structures alluded to earlier in Bach's *St. Ann's Fugue* that inspired Schoenberg to transcribe this organ fugue and its preceding prelude for a huge orchestra. For most of the generally homophonic textures of the prelude, Schoenberg combined the various orchestral choirs, using a wide range of timbral blends. In the fugue, by contrast, the emphasis is more on separate timbres for various strata. The first section ($\frac{4}{2}$), for instance, is scored entirely for winds (including horns), with the clarinet choir alone carrying the entire fugal exposition. The strings present the opening of the second section (in $\frac{6}{4}$). Later portions use a wider range of timbral contrast. In the final section of the fugue, the contrast between the sixteenth-note motion and the now cantus-

5–12. Schoenberg, *Chamber Symphony*, op. 9

5–12. (Continued)

5–13. Schoenberg, *Chamber Symphony No. 1*, op. 9

firmus-like opening subject is highlighted by timbral contrasts and by doublings that emphasize the registral separation of the individual textural strands. As a result, the diverse levels of activity are projected with a clarity not possible in the more unified timbres of an organ.

152

MULTIPLE METRIC LEVELS AND TEXTURE

It should be clear by this point that the mere presence of rhythmic activity on many levels of a metric hierarchy does not by itself create multiple interacting levels of essential motion. The openings of Mozart's *Symphony No. 40* and Beethoven's *Symphony No. 5*, for instance, offer as many levels of activity as Bach's *C-Minor Fugue (Well-Tempered Clavier, I)* and *Ab-Major Prelude (Well-Tempered Clavier, II)*. Yet, as shown in chapter 3 and earlier in this chapter, the Mozart and Beethoven passages have a single indisputable primary metric level, while it is possible to argue for either of two primary metric levels in the Bach excerpts.

The occurrence of such multiple levels requires that some essential musical component (or several essential components) carries on activity at more than one level. The component may be caused by harmonic changes (as in Bach's *C-Minor Fugue;* review examples 5-1 through 5-3), phrasing length (as in Mahler's *Symphony No. 3;* review examples 5-10 and 5-11), or grouping or patterning (as in Brahms' *Intermezzo,* op. 119, no. 2; review example 5-7).

The compositional attitudes that allow or do not allow multiple pacings to arise lie deep in the style of an era or of a composer. Edward Cone notes the primacy of the beat as a basic metric unit in Bach's music.[8] He contrasts this with the primacy of the measure or of the four-measure phrase in tonal music of later eras. From our current perspective, Cone's insistence on the primary of the beat in Bach's music goes a long way toward explaining the multiple levels present in much of his music. The ever-articulated beat and its subdivisions provide one level, while the measure or two-measure level provides the other. Bach's sixteenths, for instance, are rarely a mere stream of activity filling the space between downbeats; they are far more often one focus of attention.

As we observed in comparing Bach's and Schumann's accompaniments to the *E-Major Preludio* (review example 5-5), and as we noted in connection with Gounod's *Ave Maria,* it is not only the presence of articulated sixteenth-note motion that produces the multiple levels. It is the texture, with articulations of all levels and the interactions between these levels, that creates the multileveled vitality of Bach's works. And this interaction between levels is what permeates Bach's counterpoint. Throughout his works, Bach created textures in which multiple levels of pacing abound. It is the essence of his contrapuntal voice leading. And it is present even in his homophonic textures (as, for instance, in the sinfonia to *Cantata No. 29*).

It was against this very aspect of High-Baroque music that the pre-Classical composers rebeled. In seeking to avoid textural density, they concentrated on clear presentation of melodic lines in predominantly homophonic textures. Vocal styles were a powerful influence.[9] The motor-rhythm beat subdivisions became accompanimental, supporting the larger phrase shape without adding a new level of essential activity. The propulsive figured bass gave way to a supportive bass marking off chord changes or activating time spans just like any other accompanimental part.

The misconception that Classic and Romantic music lacks counterpoint is popular, but it is a misconception nonetheless. As Schenker demonstrated, counterpoint is the core of all tonal music. Post-Baroque contrapuntal textures differ from Baroque ones for rhythmic reasons, not because of a lack of voice-leading techniques. Most post-Baroque composers were capable of composing a convincing fugato or double counterpoint when they desired— including even multiple rhythmic levels in the Bachian sense. But this was not as overriding a concern for them on a regular basis as it was for Bach. And often their fugatos and other polyphonic passages convey a somewhat strained, artificial, and even academic character. Think of the fugatos in Schubert's *Wanderer Fantasy*, or in Saint-Saens' *Danse Macabre*. Even in such masterpieces as the finale of the *Eroica*, the finale of Mozart's *String Quartet*, K. 387, or some of the fugal movements in the late works of Beethoven, the polyphonic web frequently gives way to the homophonic textures more characteristic of those eras. Perhaps nowhere is the dichotomy of a fugal/contrapuntal style and a personal style more clearcut than in Schumann's *Four Fugues* for piano, op. 72. In the fourth fugue, Schumann puts the four-measure subject through its paces for some sixty measures in strict four-part writing. The subject or its parts dominate every measure, replete with numerous strettos. Then after a more Schumannesque, but still polyphonic, passage (measures 61–69), the six measures in example 5-14, labeled "coda," conclude the piece with vintage Schumann.

Only in the late nineteenth century does counterpoint featuring truly independent pacings (akin to the excerpts discussed in Mahler's *Third Symphony*) reappear. In that music, the simultaneous pacings are not nested within one another but point to diver-

Im mässigen Tempo (♩ = 104)

5–14. Schumann, *Four Fugues*, op. 72, no. 4

gent simultaneous musics, providing another of the internal forces that weakened the bonds of functional tonality in the late nineteenth century.

In addition to already cited instances, see the prelude to act 1 of Wagner's *Meistersinger* (example 5-15). Beginning in measure 158, the musical fabric consists entirely of previously stated themes, each with its own character, and each moving at its own pace. Re-

5–15. Wagner, *Die Meistersinger von Nürnberg, Vorspiel*

markable even for Wagner is the specificity with which he notates the character of each textural strand. Is this passage a typically Wagnerian dramatic-psychological interpretation of the interaction of various plots and subplots as represented by the leitmotifs? Or is this another one of the parodies of the opera—a sort of purposefully pedantic musical nonsense in which the counterpoint works intervallically, but the lines really do not belong together?

Or what is one's reaction to the juxtaposition of two separate and differently paced themes in Fritz Kreisler's cadenza to the first movement of the Beethoven *Violin Concerto* (example 5–16)?

5–16. Kreisler, *Cadenza* to first movement of Beethoven's
Violin Concerto, op. 61

Tovey called this combination "ingenious," but doubted that Beethoven would have ever thought of it.[10] Is there any comparable pairing of differently paced themes in Beethoven's output? Or is this a juxtaposition that only one living outside of Beethoven's stylistic world could have dreamt of?

6

HYPERMETER, METER, AND PHRASE RHYTHMS

No aspect of tonal rhythmic theory has aroused more controversy than the existence and nature of metric organization above the level of the notated measure. Theorists differ over the existence of meter at ever-higher levels of structure. And even those theorists who agree on the existence of metric organization at a given level of structure may disagree about its nature—whether it is like metric organization within the measure, or whether it is of a different character altogether. Depending on their position concerning these issues, theorists differ in interpreting the accentual status of phrase beginnings and of cadences. There is a close bond between all of these issues and important aspects of musical performance.

In much of the theoretical literature on rhythm, positions concerning hypermeter have been defended or assailed more often by assertions and by appeals to authority (with Nature often lurking in the background as the ultimate authority) than by a careful consideration of the issues and the implications of various positions. A plausible statement in defense of a position may, on further consideration, entail unforeseen and sometimes undesirable implications. In an attempt to avoid some of these problems of other investigations, this chapter reviews the nature of meter before considering hypermeter and phrase rhythm. In the ensuing discussions, the emphasis is more on exploring various positions than on asserting a single solution to problems. Some aspects of hypermeter and phrase rhythm have been explored most systematically by Schenkerian theorists. These issues, while mentioned in this chapter, receive a more complete discussion in chapter 7.

METER AND HYPERMETER

Meter as a Grouping of Pulses. Meter is by definition an organization of pulses that are of functionally equivalent duration (review chapter 3). For a meter, and, by extension, a hypermeter, to exist, there must be a stream of pulses to be organized. If a theorist discusses hypermetric organization other than as a grouping of pulses, that theorist is not discussing meter per se, but rather some other aspect of rhythmic structure.

Consider, for instance, Schenker's metric analysis of the opening of the scherzo of Beethoven's *Symphony No. 5* in example 6-1.[1] Schenker notes the expansion *(Dehnung)* in the second phrase by not numbering what he considers the expanded or interpolated measures. For Schenker, the hypermetric structure of a phrase is akin to the metric structure of a measure.[2] So in effect, Schenker's measure 3 of the second phrase is three times as long as any other numbered measure-pulse or hyperbeat. Schenker analyzes similar expansions in Mozart's *Symphony No. 35*,[3] Beethoven's *String Quartet,* op. 59, no. 3,[4] and other passages. At the opening of the first movement of the Beethoven string quartet, Schenker analyzes a four-unit phrase as a single hypermeasure, with beat 1 five measures long, beat 2 six measures long, and beats 3 and 4 one measure each (see example 6–2).

These imaginative and insightful analyses of Schenker's illustrate the pacing of these passages, the parallelisms among related

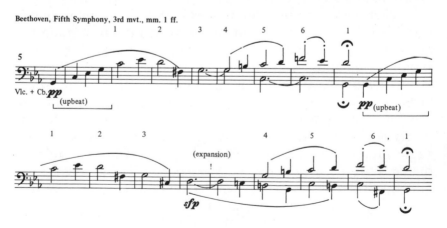

Beethoven, Fifth Symphony, 3rd mvt., mm. 1 ff.

6–1. Schenker, *Free Composition,* fig. 146/5

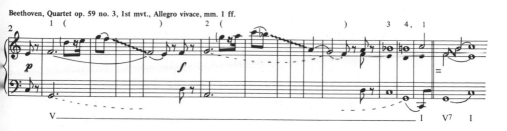

Beethoven, Quartet op. 59 no. 3, 1st mvt., Allegro vivace, mm. 1 ff.

6–2. Schenker, *Free Composition*, fig. 148/2

phrases of different lengths, and the underlying harmonic rhythm or rhythm of structural events. But they are not metric analyses in the sense that we apply the term metric to measures or to sub-measure units. Imagine how Schenker's analyses would look if the rhythmic values were reduced so that each phrase were notated as a measure as in example 6-3. Measures like these do not exist in tonal music.

Hypermeter, if it is to be analogous to meter, must concern it-self with groupings of equivalent pulses, not with the pacing of structural events—a related, but clearly separate phenomenon.

The Factors That Group Pulses. As demonstrated in chapter 3, harmonic change is the single most powerful factor that can create a metric grouping of pulses. Above or below the level(s) at which har-

or:

6–3. Possible renotations of example 6–2?

monic changes occur, durational accents and textural accents are the factors most capable of projecting metric groupings.

Pattern length helps define the length of metric units but cannot indicate the location of accents within those units. (Review example 2-35.) At and below the primary metric level, patterns refer to motives. At the hypermetric levels, patterns refer to phrases or sections. Just as the length of a motive does not indicate its internal accentuation, the length of a phrase cannot, by itself, determine its internal accentuation. The beginning of a phrase may receive a pattern-beginning accent. But that pattern-beginning accent may not necessarily occur on a metric accent.

The factors that determine meter are most effective at or below the primary metric level. Harmonic changes, durational accents, and textural accents are not often available to determine hypermetric structure. As a result, metric ambiguity (as defined in chapter 4), which is virtually unknown at the beat level and rather uncommon up to the primary metric level, becomes the norm at hypermetric levels. Only in cases in which a primary metric level exists above the level of the notated measure is an unambiguous hypermeter present.

Unambiguous Hypermeters. We have already encountered passages and entire movements in which the notated measure functions as a single beat and in which harmonic changes, durational accents, and textural accents establish multimeasure groupings as the primary metric level. Review, for instance, the discussion in chapter 3 concerning the opening of Beethoven's *Symphony No. 5.* After the two opening fermatas, four-measure hypermeasures are established by harmonic changes and persist until the fermata in measure 24. Beginning with measure 26, four-measure hypermeasures reappear. Although four-measure hypermeasures do not continue through measures 38–43, two-measure hypermeasures exist throughout this passage—coalescing into four-measure groupings again for a while after measure 44.

As already discussed in chapters 3 and 4, such hypermeters are common in scherzos, stylized dances, and other fast movements. If the hypermeter remains regular throughout the movement, the fact that the hypermeter exists may be the result of notational conventions. (Chopin's *Prelude in A Major,* op. 28, no. 7, for instance, is like many waltzes, and might have been notated in $\frac{6}{4}$, except for the fact that waltzes are conventionally notated in $\frac{3}{4}$.) But if the hypermeter changes during the course of the movement, then notating the measure as a beat at the primary metric level may have been the only possible notation for eighteenth and early nineteenth-century music. Review the discussions in chapters 3 and 4 of the first movement of Beethoven's *Fifth* and the scherzo of his *Seventh Symphony*.

Unambiguous hypermeters can also occur when the notated measure is indeed the functional measure at the primary metric level, but a higher level of meter appears temporarily. At the very opening of Mozart's *Fortieth,* for instance, the harmonic changes that occur every other measure establish a two-measure hypermeter that lasts at least through measure 9. (Review example 3-22.) At the very opening of the movement, either the measure level or the two-measure level might be heard as the primary metric level. But after measure 9, the harmonies change every measure. When two-measure harmonic changes resume after measure 20, the harmonies last from even-numbered measures through odd-numbered measures (20–21, 22–23, 24–25) in contrast to the odd-even pairings in measures 1–8 (1–2, 3–4, 5–6, 7–8). At some point(s) in measures 9–19, the two-measure level is interrupted by a change in structure. The two-measure hypermetric level recurs intermittently during the movement, but the measure remains a true meter throughout.

Another movement with a similar interaction between a continuous primary metric level and an interrupted hypermeter is the first movement of Schumann's *Symphony No. 3* (the "Rhenish"). The two-measure level is the primary metric level throughout the movement. At the very opening and in many later passages, the four-measure level is a regular hypermeter.

The Upper Limit of Unambiguous Hypermeters. For any given passage, there is a level above which a hypermeter is not definitively established. Either because the primary meter-causing factors (harmonic change, durational accents, and textural accents) do not operate at that level, or because there is no regular pulse, a hypermeter cannot be unambiguously asserted. At the very opening of Mozart's *Fortieth,* for instance, this occurs at the four-measure level. No meter-producing factors can assist us in defending either option in example 6-4.

It is at this level—the level above which the meter-producing factors operate—that musicians disagree with each other about the metric status of measures and hypermeasures. As a general rule, all musicians will agree on the metric status of any given beat subdivi-

6–4

sion (for example, the metric status of any given sixteenth or eighth in $\frac{4}{4}$ meter). And they will agree on the metric status of beats within a measure (except perhaps in the case of compound meters, in which one half of the notated measure functions as a measure on the primary metric level). And where primary meter-producing factors operate at the two-measure or four-measure level, as in the just-discussed Mozart and Beethoven excerpts, musicians will probably agree on that hypermeter.

Above that level, the disagreements seem irreconcilable. Some theorists, among them Schenker, Schachter, and Berry, have argued that hypermeter is by nature similar in structure to meter at the measure level, although with some flexibility in terms of expansions and contractions. For these theorists, the cadence to a phrase falls within the hypermeasure as the last and weakest hyperbeat. Komar argues for hypermetric structure akin to measures, but differs from Schenker, Schachter, and Berry in placing cadences at the beginnings of hypermeasures—that is, on the strongest beat. Conc argues that at some level above the primary metric level "meter must yield to a more organic rhythmic principle."[5] Cone argues that phrases tend to be accented at their beginnings and their ends, allowing the accented concluding measure of a phrase to stand next to the accented beginning measure of the next phrase. In any meter, two accented beats cannot stand next to one another. Westergaard's linear analyses reflect a viewpoint similar to Cone's.

The positions held by these theorists differ on three principal issues: the level at which meter ceases to operate, whether phrases are akin to measures in structure, and the accentual nature of cadences. Since a position on the first of these issues depends upon the other two, this chapter concerns itself primarily with the second two issues.

The Measure as a Model for Phrase Structure. Schenker, Schachter, and Berry consider the metric organization of a measure the model for the hypermetric organization of a phrase. A four-measure phrase, for instance, to them is akin to a four-beat measure, with each measure of the phrase functioning as a hyperbeat. From this perspective, they argue that the cadential measure of the phrase is inherently unaccented, occupying the least-accented portion of the hypermeasure. Schachter writes: "I see no reason to believe that the metrical organization of a group of measures differs in principle from that of a single measure and assume that both are beginning- rather than end-accented."[6] Schenker writes that "every metric scheme is capable of enclosing the cadence within itself in such a way that the [cadential] I appears in the final unaccented measure of the measure group."[7] Berry does not specifically describe phrases in general as metric units, but he does cite a Haydn phrase "as a metric unit analogous to that of the level of the notated measure,"[8] and he does notate various examples with metrically reduced values in a hypermetric scheme.[9]

But facile comparisons between measures and phrases overlook three fundamental distinctions between these categories. First, accents within a measure both recede from the preceding downbeat and also lead toward the following downbeat; such is not the case with the accentual status of measures within a phrase. Second, phrases are discrete musical thoughts, ending with a cadence and a breath that separates them from the following music. Measures are, by and large, not separate units; within a phrase they often lead directly to the following measure. Third, the accentual status of beats in a measure arises from predictably repetitious patterning. Since phrase lengths generally do not remain the same throughout most tonal pieces, there is no equivalent patterning on the phrase level. Each of these considerations merits some discussion.

Consider the accentual structure of a measure. We often think of a notated measure as an accentual structure whose lesser accents recede from the strong beats on various levels. In $\frac{4}{4}$, for instance, the second half of the measure begins with an accent less strong than the first half. The accents on the second and fourth quarters recede from the preceding stronger beat. Since the fourth beat recedes from the third beat, and the third beat itself recedes from the first beat, the fourth beat is the weakest or most recessive beat in the measure.

But in fact this is rarely the only aspect of metric accentuation in a measure. For measures do not occur singly. When measures follow one another, the music of one measure connects to the music of the next. As the previous downbeat recedes into the past, the accentual structure is both a series of afterbeats receding from that downbeat, and a series of ever-stronger upbeats leading to the next downbeat. (Schenker, in figure 140 of *Free Composition*, depicts a range of afterbeat-upbeat interactions.) Only in the very final measure of a movement, a section, or a phrase, does a final beat function solely as a point receding from the preceding downbeat.

Consider the opening of Mozart's *Piano Sonata*, K. 331, in example 6-5. The opening measures seem at first glance to be a clear-cut instance of a passage in which the music following the strong beats is recessive from those strong beats. Leonard Meyer argues for a trochaic (accented-afterbeat) grouping within each half-measure in measures 1–3.[10] And according to both traditional harmonic analysis and Schenkerian analysis, the second halves of measures 1 and 2 rebound off the downbeats of those measures.

Yet at the same time, other factors promote the ends of each measure as a forward-moving gesture leading to the following measure. From a linear perspective, the melodic E in measure 1 leads to the D in measure 2, which in turn leads to the C♯ in measure 4. (This is true whether one hears the phrase as a descent from scale-step 5, as Schenker does, or as a descent from scale-step 3, as Cone and other theorists do.[11]) Schenker's imaginative analytic slurring, shown in example 6-6, illustrates the counterpoise of these factors. The hooked slurs show the accentually recessive arpeggiation within measures 1 and 2, while the larger slur above shows the linear continuity across the four opening measures.

Common performance practice also demonstrates the rhythmic and accentual continuity in these Mozart measures. Although

6–5. Mozart, *Piano Sonata*, K. 331, first movement

6–6. Schenker, *Free Composition*, Fig. 141d

performers commonly take a short breath at the end of the end of the first phrase (end of measure 4), no such pause is effective at the end of measures 1 and 2. Indeed, executing a pause, however brief, at the end of measures 1 and 2 in order to prevent the ends of these measures from becoming upbeats to measures 2 and 3 robs the phrase of its flow. Executing a pause, however brief, at the end of each half-measure (to insure that only the trochaic grouping projects) creates a similarly stilted effect.

There is an equilibrium in this phrase between the accent-afterbeat and the upbeat-accent aspects that persists until measure 4. Only in the cadential measure does one aspect exclude the other. The harmonic change, the textural accent reinforced by a dynamic accent, and the continuity of the melodic sixteenths make the third eighth of measure 4 exclusively an upbeat to the second half of the measure. And the final eighth of the measure, as the cadence of the phrase, is exclusively an afterbeat.

It is this dual aspect of metric accentuation at and below the measure level that becomes problematic when a metric hypermeter is assumed at the phrase level. None of the theorists who argue for metric hypermeter at the phrase level addresses this issue. But I do not believe that they would argue for the type of metric continuity at the phrase level that is all but ubiquitous at the measure level. Do measures 2, 3, and 4 of Mozart's variations theme (or of any such phrase) become increasingly strong "hyperupbeats" to the second phrase? Hardly. And the reason is that at the phrase level, sectional divisions take on a different character than they do below the phrase level. Measures, beats, beat divisions, and beat subdivisions are segments of longer units, while a phrase is a complete entity. This aspect of a phrase is universally recognized by musicians when they define a phrase in terms of a complete musical thought. Traditional harmonic theorists note the requirement of a fundamental harmonic progression (a "cadence formula") to mark off the ending of a phrase; linear theorists note the composing-out of a linear span as the structural essence of a phrase.[12] And performers routinely breathe between phrases, setting off the end of a phrase from the beginning of the next phrase. But they rarely, if ever, articulate the end of a measure within a phrase in the same way.

Perhaps the most striking way of demonstrating the difference between a regular hypermeter and nonmetric phrase structure is to compare a phrase like the Mozart passage (or nearly any phrase from tonal music) with music that really demonstrates several levels of regular hypermeter, as much of the music of Bruckner does. Many movements of his feature several levels of a regular hypermeter. Example 6-7 is a durational reduction of the opening of his *Symphony No. 4.* After the two opening measures, the measures group into fours, and the four-groupings themselves are in groups of fours. Even at this hypermetric level (where the pulse is four measures of music), the structure is akin to beats within a measure. The four-measure groups are all open-ended; each flows without any cadential articulation into the next hypermeasure. There is a strong elided cadence to the section—at letter A on the strong beat of the sixteen-measure hypermeter level. Here, the hypermeter truly is a meter. And how unlike the Mozart phrase or nearly any other tonal phrase this structure is!

Deryck Cooke, in his perceptive essay on Bruckner in *The New Grove,* comments on the singular sense of form and continuity in Bruckner's music.

. . . [Bruckner's] extraordinary attitude to the world, and the nature of his materials which arose from this attitude, dictated an entirely unorthodox handling of traditional formal procedures. Sonata form is a dynamic, hymanistic process, always going somewhere, constantly trying to arrive; but with Bruckner firm in his religious faith, the music has no need to go anywhere, no need to find a point of arrival, because it is already there. The various stages of the formal process are not offered as dynamic phases of a drama, but as so many different viewpoints from which to absorb the basic material. The stance is not Romantic, but medieval; indeed, the mentality of the Austrian Catholic peasantry, which Bruckner to a very large extent retained, was essentially a survival from the Middle Ages. Experiencing Bruckner's symphonic music is more like walking around a cathedral, and taking in each aspect of it, than like setting out on a journey to some hoped-for goal.[13]

I do not believe that those theorists who argue that phrase structure is akin to metric structure in most eighteenth- and nineteenth-

6–7. Bruckner, *Symphony No. 4,* first movement. All rhythmic values reduced to ¹/₄ of original. Measure numbers are those of the original notation. Original meter signature is ₵.

century music believe that this music is like Bruckner's, rhythmically.

Meter as a Measurement of Time. Within the measure and at all lower levels of the metric hierarchy, meter locates points and spans in time in relation to the accented and unaccented beats. It is because of the metric hierarchy that we can say that a given note or harmony is an anticipation, a delay, a syncopation, an upbeat, an afterbeat, and so forth. That we can make such assertions is the result of both the regularity of meter and the clear-cut accentual structure of each level of the metric hierarchy. In $\frac{4}{4}$ meter, for example, we not only know that the measure is four beats long. We also know that beat 1 is the primary beat of the measure, beat 3 is a lesser accent, beats 2 and 4 are still weaker accents, and the subdivisions of these beats are weaker still. In identifying a note or other event as beginning on, say, the third beat of the measure, or on the eighth before beat 4, we place that note or event in a specific durational and accentual position in the metric hierarchy, a position in relation to both the preceding and the following events.

Identifying an event as occurring at a specific point in a phrase does not carry the same import. Measures and measure subdivisions are of predictable length and accentual structure because of their incessant repetition. Phrases are, in most tonal music, of varying length. Recognizing that an event occurs on, say, the third measure of a phrase, or the upbeat to the fourth measure, does not specify where that event is in relation to preceding and following accented points. The phrase may be of a different number of measures than the previous phrase(s), it may begin with one or more upbeat measures, and it may feature an irregular accentual pattern.

Even where there is a demonstrably regular hypermetric structure several levels above the primary metric level, the question remains of how this large-scale regularity is perceived. Meter is the grouping of pulses. We, as listeners, internalize perceived pulses, whether or not we actually tap a foot or move physically to the music. At some level, units simply become too long to be perceived as single pulses awaiting a higher level of grouping. In Bruckner's *Symphony No. 4,* for instance, consciously following the four-measure, the eight-measure, and even the sixteen-measure pulses is surely one way to make this music maddeningly uninteresting. For in order to perceive these large units as pulses, we, as listeners, must suppress somewhat their status as groupings of lower-level pulses. (Review the discussion of Bach's *Prelude in A♭ Major* in chapter 3 [example 3-24]. The tempo at which the piece is taken determines to some extent which metric regularities are brought into focus.) This is not to say that we do not recognize the large-scale regularity in this or other music, but rather to suggest that we may perceive this large-scale regularity as something other than meter in the sense that we mean meter at the measure level. As a result of the preceding discussion, it is clear that the accentual status of the measure cannot provide a model for accentuation within phrases.

Accentual Status of Cadences. Also bearing on the subject of hypermeter are a given theorist's thoughts about the accentual status of cadences. Sessions, Cone, and others regard cadences as inherently strong "in order to produce a sense of closure."[14] Schenker and many of his disciples, as well as Berry, insist that cadences are inherently unaccented. Schenker bases this position on his assertion that phrase structure is essentially metric. "Unless there are rhythmic demands to the contrary, every metric scheme is capable of enclosing the cadence within itself in such a way that the I appears in the final unaccented measure of the measure group."[15]

Berry is even more emphatic: ". . . the ultimate cadential event *is recessive at all but the mensural and lower levels of metric structure.* A great deal of distortion in musical performance is accountable, we believe, to failure to appreciate this usual metric function of cadential arrival."[16] For Berry, "progressive and recessive (intensifying and resolving) processes are seen as basic to musical effect and experience."[17] Since cadential arrival usually resolves preceding harmonies and brings linear spans to their close, cadences must be recessive by nature.[18] When an elision joins the cadential arrival of one phrase with the beginning of the next, "the inherently weak conclusive [impulse] assumes vicariously the accentual strength of an imposed initiative [impulse]."[19]

Granting the axiomatic assertions about progressive and recessive (intensifying and resolving) processes, one can still question Berry's additional assumption that accent and resolution are inherently contradictory. Sessions, after all, uses a similar analogy ("the alternation of cumulative tension with its release") to argue that the point of release, the cadence, is inherently accented.[20] Furthermore, upbeats resolve on their accented conclusions. Resolution of harmonic, linear, and rhythmic processes can be an affirmative process, the arrival on a goal, not merely the retreat from the preceding intensity. Thus, even if one wishes to view music from Berry's progressive-recessive perspective, one does not have to accept cadences as inherently unaccented in the hypermeter.

Regardless of such systematic considerations, listen to the opening of the slow movement of Mozart's *Piano Concerto,* K. 503, in example 6-8. By all the accentual criteria that create metric accents, this four-measure phrase is weak-strong-weak-strong. The

6–8. Mozart, *Piano Concerto,* K. 503, second movement

harmonic changes in measures 2 and 4, the durational accents on measures 2 and 4, the powerful textural accent on measure 2 (reinforced dynamically), and another textural accent on measure 4 all

170

work in concert. The slurs in the bass part and horns between measures 2 and 3 mitigate against any strong accent beginning measure 3.

Following the opening tutti, the solo piano presentation of this phrase (measures 23–26) offers the same accentual profile. But quite a different situation arises at the beginning of the recapitulation (measures 74–77). The first measure of the phrase is now the tonic resolution of a fifteen-measure dominant pedal. The last four measures of this pedal feature a series of suspensions in the upper voices that pile up on top of each other in an increasingly complex fashion before converging on measure 74 (example 6-9).

Because of the preceding music, then, the first measure of the phrase beginning in measure 74 is strong. But the accentual profile of the phrase itself is the same as on its two earlier appearances (measures 1–4 and 23–26).[21]

The beginning of this recapitulation is the reverse of what Berry assumes is the usual situation in a phrasing elision. Berry, as just noted, argues that cadences are by nature metrically weak and become strong in phrasing elisions by vicariously partaking of the accent that begins the next phrase. In this Mozart recapitulation, the harmonic change (measure 74) that culminates the dominant pedal is, by the criteria of harmonic change and textural accents, metrically strong. But it partakes vicariously in the metric *weakness* of the opening of the four-measure phrase as this phrase unfolds with its accented second and fourth measures.

This passage should not be regarded as the proverbial exception that supposedly proves the rule. For above the primary metric level, the rule is a paucity of accentual criteria that can support any single delineation of metric accents. This is especially true at cadences. Two of the primary meter-causing factors, harmonic change and durational accents, only rarely operate above the primary metric level at phrase endings. Since a cadential progression involves two harmonies, and since the flow of continuity toward the end of a phrase usually involves fairly frequent harmonic changes, harmonies most often change at least once every real measure at phrase endings. And since a long duration or a long pause following the arrival on the cadential goal or on the penultimate harmony would halt the continuity of the phrase, decisive durational accents usually do not come into play at cadences.

As a result, textural accent is the only one of the primary meter-producing factors that can commonly be effective at the ends

6–9. Mozart, *Piano Concerto*, K. 503, second movement

of phrases. Textural accents come into play at cadences when a phrase features texturally similar music until the arrival on the cadential chord itself. See example 6-10 for several instances. In the

6–9. *(Continued)*

Haydn phrase, for instance, the arrival on a denser voicing in measure 8, reinforced by the entry of the viola, and by the arrival on a
new harmony after the syncopated linear and harmonic sequence

6–9. (Continued)

that prolongs I in measures 4–7, causes a pronounced textural accent on measure 8, an accent noticeable in all recordings of this work.

6–9. *(Continued)*

In triple meters, the frequent presence of hemiola immediately before cadences precludes any accent at all in the penultimate measure of the phrase, thereby strengthening the textural accent on the

Haydn, *Symphony No. 104,* first movement, allegro

Mozart, *Piano Sonata,* K. 284, third movement

Beethoven, *Piano Sonata,* op. 2, no. 1, second movement

6–10

final cadential arrival. Indeed, the extent to which hemiola is a pre-cadential phenomenon in many stylized dance forms may be traced to the desire for a clear projection of accented cadential arrivals.

A final consideration that affects the accentual status of cadences is a given theorist's attitude toward hierarchical linear analysis (Schenkerian analysis). The first and last chords of a phrase are generally the two most background events in that phrase. Those theorists who equate more background status with greater accent, therefore, conceive of cadences as occurring on an accented measure within the phrase. Since several aspects of this issue are special to linear analysis, it is discussed in greater detail in chapter 7.

Cadences are by nature neither metrically accented nor metrically unaccented. As is the case with any other point in a phrase, their accentual status is created by their context—by the preceding patterns of accentuation and by the accent-producing factors that occur along with them. As discussed earlier in this chapter, and as demonstrated in a number of analyses later in this chapter, it is more important to assess the interpretative effects of an accented or unaccented cadence on a passage than to assert a single status for cadences as a general rule.

Hypermeter versus Nonmetric Structures. The aim of the preceding discussion in this chapter is not to assert a single approach to hypermeter. Rather, the purpose is to point out some problems and some implications of various approaches to this issue. The absence of meter-producing factors much above the primary metric level precludes any definitive conclusions concerning these issues. One can assert and find some basis for any of several large-scale accentual patterns in most musical passages. The most beneficial approach is probably not to impose any prior scheme upon a passage as a general rule, but rather to explore every passage to uncover the vibrant interaction of accentual patterns that lie within most tonal music.

The remainder of this chapter explores accentuations in several excerpts and discusses the implications of differing approaches for performers and listeners.

PHRASE RHYTHMS

Even in music that seems at first glance to exhibit regular groupings and to imply a regular hypermeter, other accentual factors are often at play. Consider the passage in example 6-11—the sixteen-measure parallel period that both begins and concludes Chopin's *Mazurka,* op. 67, no. 3. As in most of Chopin's mazurkas, and, indeed, in much stylized dance music, pairs of measures form the building blocks of phrases. Based on the melodic patterning and the phrase groupings, the period is structured as follows:

$$(2 + 2) \quad + 4//(2 + 2) \quad + 4//:\| \quad \text{seq} = \text{sequence}$$

seq   seq

imperf.   perfect

cadence   cadence

Pairs of measures group into fours, fours into eights, and eights into sixteen. The sixteen-measure period is repeated, forming a thirty-two-measure opening section for this piece.

Certainly the passage can be heard in a duple hypermeter. The motivic patterning, the change of harmony in measure 5 of each phrase, and the new texture at the beginning of each phrase, all support this option. If a duple hypermeter is heard, the cadential $^6_4$ to

6–11. Chopin, *Mazurka,* op. 67, no. 3

178

dominant in measures 6–7 of each phrase begins on an unaccented measure. Both Schachter and Komar take note of unaccented cadential $^6_4$'s in similar contexts. Schachter calls them anticipating $^6_4$'s and cites Chopin as one composer who employs them.[22] Komar cites a Chopin waltz as his example of this type of progression.[23]

But to my ears, this mode of hearing results in a rather sing-song conception of the passage. The point here, it seems to me, is that this mazurka, like so many other examples of art music based on stylized dances, displays a remarkable degree of accentual and structural freedom within the confines imposed by its genre. Several factors in this mazurka point to an accentual structure other than the alternation of strong and weak measures.

Consider first the cadential $^6_4$'s in each phrase. They arrive in the sixth measures; and there is no melodic articulation at all on the downbeats of measure 7 of each phrase when the resolution to V_7 takes place. Also note the left-hand rest on the third beat of measures 5 and 13—the only interruptions in the ♩ 𝆕 𝆕 accompanimental pattern. Because of this rest, there is a stronger textural accent on measures 6 and 14 (the arrivals on the cadential $^6_4$) than on any other internal measure in the period. Measure 6, therefore, is accented by texture and harmonic change (the arrival on the two-measure dominant)—two of the three primary meter-producing factors. Measure 7 receives no accentuations from any meter-producing factor. Only a willful insistence on a duple hypermeter allows a listener to suppress the accent on measure 6 and add the "oomph" to make measure 7 accentually stronger than measure 6.

Consider also how unlike an ordinary cadence the phrase-ending in measure 8 is. The first phrase clearly projects a tonic-supported E ($\hat{3}$), rearticulated over the cadential $^6_4$ and descending to a dominant-supported D ($\hat{2}$) in measure 7. The same structure recurs in the consequent phrase with a conclusive descent to C ($\hat{1}$). (The opening four measures of each phrase foreshadow the overall $\hat{3}$-$\hat{2}$-$\hat{1}$ structural motion in diminution over the tonic pedal. This diminution is reinforced at the lower octave by the upper notes of the left-hand part and includes the chromatic lower neighbor to D that recurs in the larger structural progression.)

But what is the status of measure 8? To what note does the D ($\hat{2}$) from measure 7 progress as the tonic harmony arrives? To the melodic G in measure 8? That would give rise to outer-voice parallel fifths (D/G to G/C) during the V_7-I progression. Is the period an instance of interruption, but with the tonic harmony arriving one measure too early: at the end of the first phrase instead of at the beginning of the second phrase? Or is it that the first phrase prolongs E, and the melody note that belongs over measure 8—the E—does not occur until measure 9? In either interpretation, the repeated tonic in measures 8–9 and the melodic E in measure 9 that continues the melodic structure broken off after measure 7 weaken the sense of a new beginning at the opening of the consequent phrase.

As a result of these accentual and structural factors, a rather more complex accentuation exists here than a simple duple hypermeter. Example 6-12 suggests two alternatives that differ in their interpretation of the connection between the antecedent and consequent phrases. Neither presents a complete picture of articulation within the passage, since neither includes the duple pairing caused by the patterns and melodic motives noted earlier. It is the composite of all these accentuations and groupings that is the large-scale rhythm of this passage.

Lest any doubts remain that a regular duple hypermeter is but a pale way to hear this Chopin excerpt, compare the music to the period in example 6-13. Like the first phrase of the Chopin, this per-

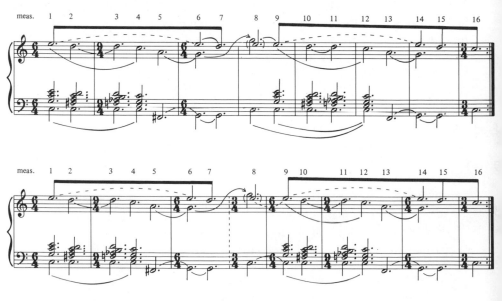

6–12

iod is eight measures long, is in $\frac{3}{4}$ meter, ends with an imperfect cadence on the tonic, features pairs of measures as building blocks, and is in pretty much the same tempo. Despite these similarities, there is a crucial difference between the rhythms of these two excerpts. In the Chopin mazurka, the primary metric level is the notated measure. In the Beethoven period, the two-measure unit is the primary metric level, established by harmonic changes. So unlike the Chopin phrase just discussed, a regular alternation of strong-weak measures persists here—reinforced by the arrival on the final harmony of each phrase division in measures 3 and 7 (not in measures 4 and 8 as in the Chopin). To try to hear Chopin's phrase, in which harmonic changes every measure reinforce textural accents to establish the notated meter as the primary metric level, and in which strong accentual factors contradict pairing of measures, in the same metric structure as the Beethoven phrase, is to force the suppleness of Chopin's phrase into a Procrustean bed.

In the case of phrases containing a prime number of measures above 3, there is no question of a regular hypermeter. One such passage is the *Chorale St. Antoni* (Haydn ?)[24]—the theme upon which Brahms based his *Variations,* op. 56 (see example 6-14). The two opening phrases are five measures each. In Schenker's analysis of the first phrase, the melodic third-spans create a 3 + 2 grouping. The second phrase is analyzed in parallel fashion (example 6-15). Schenker regards this five-measure structure as arising from a four-measure hypermeter in which the first two measures become three

6–13. Beethoven, *Piano Trio,* op. 1, no. 3, first movement

6–14. *Chorale St. Antoni*

6–15. Schenker, *Free Composition*, fig. 138/3

by the "interpolation of the neighboring note in the first third-progression."[25]

A different motivic parallelism, this one in the bass, coupled with the harmonic structure of the phrase, gives rise equally well to a 2 + 3 or 2 + 2 + 1 subdivision of the opening phrase. After prolonging I for the first two measures, the bass arrives on the dominant in measure 3, supporting C in the melody. The bass then proceeds to move in a double-neighbor pattern around V: F-[F♯]-G-E♭-[E♮]-F. The dominant in measure 5 once again supports C in the melody. The moving eighths in the bass in measure 3, coupled with the faster harmonic rhythm, support measure 3 rather than measure 4 as the point at which the second phrase division begins.

Schenker's analysis makes measures 1, 4, 6, and 9 accentually

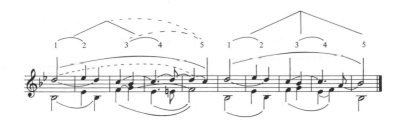

6–16

strong. (He specifically cites measure 10 as an instance of a cadential tonic in an unaccented measure.[26]) In the alternate analysis in
example 6-16, measures 1, 3, and 5, and 6, 8, and 10 are accentually
strong. Each structure is plausible from its own perspective; yet
each seems to contradict the other. From another perspective, however, there is no conflict. The primary metric level here is that of the
notated measure, established by durational accents, harmonic
changes, and textural accents. The disagreement between the 3 + 2
or 2 + 3 subdivisions is not so much a matter of metrics as it is a
matter of the direction of motions within the phrase. And from this
perspective it is not irreconcilable to have the melodic division
3 + 2 based on the thirds noted by Schenker and to have the accompanying voices, especially the bass, subdivide 2 + 3. Indeed, hearing
the phrase entirely from either point of view is not fully satisfactory.
If you hear the melody subdivided into 2 + 3, the C over the dominant arrives already in measure 3, making the next three measures
sound like an extension of an already achieved goal. And if you wish
to hear the bass and harmonies subdivided in 3 + 2, try to
imagine how the bass players would subdivide 3 + 2: Where and
how would they articulate the phrase subdivision? It is the diversity
of the overlapping subdivisions that creates the unity of the five-
measure phrase.

Conflicting pacings and subdivisions, as in the *Chorale St. Antoni,* are quite common above the primary metric level. In the five-
measure phrases of the chorale, the overlapping melodic and harmonic subdivisions create continuity within the phrase. A similar
effect is common even in even-numbered phrase structures. Listen
to the Beethoven phrase in example 6-17, *Piano Sonata,* op. 10, no.
1, second movement.

6–17. Beethoven, *Piano Sonata,* op. 10, no. 1, second movement

The 2 + 2 + 4 melodic subdivisions are as clear-cut as in the Chopin mazurka discussed earlier. Measures 1–2 and 3–4 are framed, respectively, by tonic and dominant chords. The phrasing subdivisions and apparent harmonic structure seem to support a melodic ascent to the structural C in measure 5 (example 6-18).

6–18

It would seem that the passage is a clear-cut instance of a duple hypermeter. But several factors argue against this assumption and create a more dynamic rhythm in measures 1–5. First, the primary metric level is that of the notated measure. Any larger rhythms cannot be determined by the primary meter-producing factors. Second, measures 3–4 are not parallel in structure to measures 1–2. The harmonic supports shape these measures quite differently. Measures 1–2 are framed by identically voiced root-position tonic tri-

184

ads. Measures 3–4 begin and end with dominant chords with rather different functions. The dominant in measure 3 is an inverted dominant seventh, whereas the dominant in measure 4 is a root-position triad. (For voice-leading reasons, a seventh chord would be problematic in measure 4. If the seventh were in an inner voice, its resolution would double the C in measure 5; if the chord seventh, D♭, were in the melody, it would interrupt the ascent to C and detract from the power of the subdominant later in the phrase. In either case, a seventh in measure 4 would detract from the ascent to the C in measure 5.)

The two types of dominants in measures 3 and 4 create a more complex rhythm in measures 3–4 than in measures 1–2. The inverted dominant seventh in measure 3 resolves to the following tonic, which then proceeds by root progression to the dominant in measure 4 (see example 6-19). The long appoggiatura on the second beat of measure 3 precludes the possibility that that tonic chord is the goal of the progression. Note that Beethoven's slurring supports this analysis in that it slurs measures 1–2 as a single unit but slurs measure 3 separately from measure 4. Note also the accompanimental eighths that lead to the dominant in measure 4 and cease on its arrival.

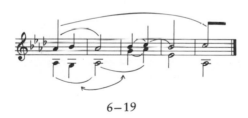

6–19

As a result, a far more dynamic rhythm exists here than a mere duple hypermeter. The harmonic motions conflict with the 2 + 2 melodic subdivisions until all arrive on the downbeat of measure 5—the goal of the opening ascent and the beginning of the structural line of the phrase. The two foreshadowings of A♭-B♭-C provide another set of anticipatory motions leading to measure 5: the A♭-B♭-[A♭-G-A♭-]C of the opening melodic turn figure and the A♭-A♮-B♭-[D♭-]C of measures 2–3. Imagine how much weaker the arrival on C in measure 5 would be if there really were more evidence of a duple hypermeter, as in example 6-20.

6–20

Hypermetric Phrase Structures. It should not be construed from the preceding discussion that regular hypermeters never function much above the level of the primary meter. An earlier section of this chapter has demonstrated their presence in works of Bruckner. Other instances commonly occur in continuous transitional or developmental passages, especially where strong cadential articulations are absent, as in example 6-21. Hypermeters also frequently occur in closing passages, either of sections or of movements, where cadences continually elide with the beginning of the next phrase (see example 6-22).

6–21. Schumann, *Symphony No. 4,* op. 120, first movement

186

6–21. *(Continued)*

6–22. Mozart, *Violin Concerto No. 3*, K. 216, end of finale

The Four-Measure Phrase as a Norm

In some musical genres and in the music of some historical periods, four-measure phrases predominate as the most frequent phrase length. As Cone has already noted, this was especially true in the nineteenth century[27]—the period when the predecessors of our contemporary ideas about musical rhythm arose. It is no accident, then,

187

that theorists as diverse as Riemann and Schenker agree that group-ings in multiples of two—especially in fours—are a norm against which other phrase lengths are to be measured. Schenker, for in-stance, argues that "since the principle of systole and diastole is in-herent in our very being, metric ordering based on two and its mul-tiples is the most natural to us. . . . Measure orderings in odd numbers (such as 3 or 5) have their roots in a duple ordering in the background and middleground."[28]

Since the notion of duple groupings as a norm is closely related to, and indeed is used as an argument for, regular hypermeters, this notion merits close examination here. That there is much music, es-pecially stylized dance music and much homophonic music, featur-ing persistent four-measure phrases is beyond dispute. The subject of the present discussion is whether this frequent occurrence means that four-measure or duple orderings are a natural or normal stand-ard for music that is not grouped in fours.

Arguments concerning the naturalness of duple rhythms in music, whether they are based on internal human rhythms (heart-beats, walking, breathing, and the like) or on the inherent nature of duple organization (tension-release, accent-nonaccent, and so forth), do not stand up to historical or cross-cultural scrutiny. Even leaving aside so-called primitive or non-Western musics that do not show a preponderance of duple metric divisions, the early history of Western art music itself demonstrates that duple meters arose after triple meters and were first defended as an inferior rhythm. Not only Jacob of Liège's conservative attack on the duple meters of the *ars nova* (*Speculum musicae,* ca. 1330), but even Jean de Muris *Ars novae musicae* (ca. 1316–1319), defending the new style, insist that only ternary meters are perfect.[29] And who wishes to argue that the waltz, the minuet, and countless other triple-meter dance genres are somehow less natural than duple-metered dances? Finally, anyone who has ever taught music to young children knows that teaching them to divide a time span into two equal parts (say, a quarter into eighths) is no easier or more natural than teaching than other simple divisions. Appeals to nature or to cosmology have been used by many theorists over the centuries to find a basis for then-current musical conventions. In all cases, changing styles have revealed the inadequacy of the appeal.

The normalcy of duple or four-measure groupings also fails to stand up to scrutiny. To be sure, numerous phrases, phrase subdivisions, and periods (pairs of phrases) are in twos, fours, eights, and sixteens. But numerous phrase groupings in the tonal repertoire contain an odd number of measures, or a multiple of an odd number ($6 = 3 \times 2$, and so forth). Other than the assertion that the duple divisions are primary and the nonduple divisions derived by expansion, interpolation, contraction, or elision, there is no reason for assuming the primacy of one type of grouping over another. Indeed, the assertion that nonduple divisions arise as adjustments in a duple framework often leads to absurd arguments. Consider the case of phrase elisions—when the cadential arrival of one phrase is the point of initiation of the next. When the cadential arrival is in the fourth or eighth measure, theorists analyze a four- or eight-measure phrase, with the fourth or eighth measure also being measure 1 of the next phrase. See example 6-23, in which the opening period would be considered 8 + 8 measures, followed by an eight-measure phrase (with subdivisions). The seven measures of the consequent phrase (measures 9–15) are analyzed as eight (measures 9–16). Twenty-three measures of music (8 + 7 + 8) are analyzed as twenty-four measures of phrases.

6–23. Haydn, *Symphony No. 104,* first movement

But when elisions result in four-measure groupings, the same reasoning is not adopted. Review the passage in example 6-22. Each phrase, counting its cadence measure, is five measures long, as noted in example 6-4. Only the elisions cause the persistent four-measure groupings here. Would those theorists who argue for the primacy of the eight-measure groupings in the Haydn *Symphony No. 104* also argue for the primacy of the five-measure phrases in the Mozart *Violin Concerto,* each phrase shortened by one measure because of elisions?

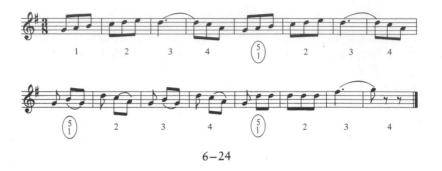

6–24

The same line of reasoning works in both passages. If the eight-measure phrases are primary in the Haydn passage, then the five-measure phrases are primary in the Mozart passage. Yet the Mozart passage is the very model of a four-measure hypermeter that functions just like a regular meter—that is, the later hyperbeats (that is, measures) in each grouping serve not only as afterbeats of the preceding downbeat, but also become upbeats to the next downbeat. If the four-measure resultant duration of each phrase in the Mozart passage is the primary division, then the seven-measure consequent phrase in the Haydn period is the primary division there. Only by accepting variable phrase lengths as equally primary and by abandoning a general assumption of four-measure phrases as a norm can this conundrum be resolved.

Schachter has argued that once we hear an antecedent phrase, we expect the consequent phrase to be of the same length and regard any differences in length as alterations. Thus, if an antecedent is four measures long, we expect four measures in the consequent.[30] Certainly there are many periods in which both the antecedent and consequent phrases are identical in length. There are also numerous thematic statements and other passages that are not in balanced pairs of phrases. One could easily argue that uneven periods are the norm, since in many movements, the balanced pairs of phrases often stand out from their irregularly-phrased context. And on a larger scale, it is rare indeed to find a binary form, even a simple one, in which the second half of the movement is the same length as the first. Since differing phrase lengths are as much the norm as identical phrase lengths, it is not apparent why we should hear consequent phrases or sections as alternations in length from the first phrase.

A final consideration argues against proceeding from the presence of four-measure groupings to the assumption of a regular hypermeter. Excerpts discussed earlier in this chapter (Chopin's *Mazurka,* op. 67, no. 3; Mozart's *Piano Concerto,* K. 503; and Beethoven's *Piano Sonata,* op. 10, no. 2) have demonstrated that four-measure phrases or phrase subdivisions do not necessarily imply a regular hypermeter. A particularly striking example opens Haydn's *String Quartet,* op. 77, no. 2 (example 6-25). The two opening phrases add up to eight measures. The first four measures clearly subdivide into twos by virtue of textural accents (reinforced by dynamic changes) and durational accents. The pacing of essential harmonic changes (omitting the changes over the pedal in measures 1–2) might even lead one to hear the two-measure unit in a

6–25. Haydn, *String Quartet,* op. 77, no. 2, first movement

191

duple hypermeter. But the next four measures are of a quite different nature. The once-a-measure harmonic changes that continue into measure 5 from 3–4 become twice-a-measure changes in measures 6–7. The resulting textural and durational accents make measure 8 a strong cadential arrival.

A different way of hearing these eight measures takes note of the motivic similarity between measures 4 and 5. Indeed, with the inverted dominant in measure 5 between the root-position tonic chords in measures 4 and 6, measure 4 can easily be heard in a dual role: as the beginning of the second phrase or as the cadence of the first phrase. From this perspective, the motivic sequence in measures 4–5 recurs in diminuted sequence in measure 6 and in further diminutions in measure 7—all leading to the cadential arrival in measure 8. The resulting structure divides the eight measures into 3 eliding into 5. The durational patterns, harmonic rhythm, motivic rhythms, composite rhythm, and other factors create a rhythmic dynamism leading to the cadential goal in measure 8, which is more the essence of the music than any regular hypermeter.

HYPERMETER AND PERFORMANCE

Questions concerning the presence, absence, or nature of hypermeter in a given passage are not of purely academic concern. How a performer projects a passage and how a listener perceives and understands that performance depend to a not insignificant extent on the issues discussed in this chapter. A person's understanding of the rhythms of a passage bears on the shaping of the musical gestures in that passage and consequently can affect such diverse aspects of performance as tone color, articulation, dynamics, rubato, and even such intangibles as lyricism and musical energy.

The shaping of gestures concerns both the articulation of segments of a piece and the connections from one segment to another on any of a number of levels. Within a phrase, for instance, it is often possible to assume one or more levels of a regular duple hypermeter above the primary metric level. But in all such excerpts introduced in this chapter, other continuities and accentuations supersede such a hypermeter as factors creating the unique shapings of time of that individual passage—shapings that are obscured or even precluded by a singsong alternation of strong and weak measures.

The metric status of cadences is another issue that concerns the articulation of segments in a piece. The extent to which a cadence is a point of arrival, concluding linear spans and harmonic motions—in short, concluding a "musical statement"—is strengthened if the cadence receives a strong metric articulation. (Of course, this may be done without playing the cadential downbeat with a loud dynamic stress.) And this cadential sense is weakened if the cadence is simply the final hyperbeat of a hypermeasure becoming an upbeat to the next hyperdownbeat.

I find it unfortunate that writings on these topics so often issue inflexible dicta about the one way to interpret a given passage or a given type of situation. For all experienced performers know that no way of performing a given piece or passage, no matter how right it seems at one time, will necessarily remain valid in a later performance. It is the variety of performance possibilities that keeps a performer interested in playing a piece time and again. Indeed, it is the ever-increasing range of possibilities that arise in the imagination of a sensitive musician that urges him or her to rework the same piece over and over again. And, conversely, it is the fact that a performer has not yet learned many of the "right" ways of performing a passage that makes both performer and audience aware of the limited possibilities of a premiere performance—whether of a new work or of a standard work new to that performer.

Berry, for instance, complains of "a great deal of distortion in musical performance" that "is accountable, we believe, to failure to appreciate [the recessive nature of] cadential arrival."[31] Certainly, overaccentuation of cadences can introduce too great a sense of arrival, and, hence, too great a sense of discontinuity with the following music. But the opposite type of performance, with wholly recessive cadences, all too often deprives a piece of the internal articulations that mark off progress through the structure and all to often leaves the end of the piece cut off without a sense of final arrival to tie the structure together.[32]

The very fact that eminent musicians—performers, composers, theorists—have found evidence to support diametrically opposing positions should lead us away from one-sided perspectives. Are we to assume that those holding views contrary to ours are wrong or unmusical? Would it not be better to assume that each side has heard a different aspect of accentuation—and then to pursue the interaction of these accentuations? Too few writings describe the range of different and often conflicting continuities that reside in any passage of more than trivial content. Probably, no single performance can ever project all the possibilities. But, all the same, no performance will succeed by projecting only one aspect of the structure.

All too often we hear theorists complaining that performers—students and professionals alike—are oblivious to theoretical perspectives. And those theorists who are also performers soon learn not to speak "theoretese" to make a point at rehearsals. Some of the reluctance of performers to pursue theoretical considerations may be attributed to ignorance. But a not insignificant aspect is the reluctance of performers to follow absolutist approaches to issues that performers know are not one-sided. Rhythm, as discussed in chapter 1, is a composite of many aspects: durational patterns, composite rhythm, the rhythms of textural changes and harmonic changes, the pacing of motives, accentuation, meter, articulation, continuity, grouping, and increases and decreases in activity in any of these aspects. As demonstrated in several analyses in this chapter, it is the composite of the many different rhythms in a given passage that opens up the range of performance possibilities of that passage. By exploring the interaction of all these factors, theorists will be better able to relate to the concerns of performers.

7

RHYTHM AND LINEAR ANALYSIS

The past generation has seen the theories of Heinrich Schenker evolve from an embattled avant-garde approach to tonal music into the lingua franca among professional theorists in North America. Schenker's writings do not include a comprehensive, explicit approach to musical rhythm. Thus, it is not surprising that several of the recent studies on rhythm explore ways to relate layer analysis and rhythmic structure. This chapter does not offer a new approach to this subject. Rather, it surveys some aspects of Schenker's and more recent writings, calling attention to some hitherto undiscussed aspects

Schenker's Approach

Schenker's own analyses often use rhythmic values in two separate ways. In all his analyses, various rhythmic symbols indicate the variety of structural meanings of notes. In addition, numerous analyses contain the actual rhythmic values of the music, helping to orient the reader and demonstrating relationships between the surface of the piece and deeper structural levels. In general, Schenker does not assert any systematic relationship between pitch processes and specific rhythmic phenomena. In those analyses that do assert such a relationship, the results raise problematic issues.

Three approaches to rhythm are implicit in Schenker's analyses. In one approach, the duration of a phrase or phrase division in the final score is accepted, and prior levels are notated so as to fit into that duration. Consider, for instance, Schenker's analysis of the subject of Bach's *Fugue in C Minor* (*Well-Tempered Clavier*, I [example 7-1]).[1] As elaborations and additional voices appear in successive levels, Schenker makes the G and F of the essential mo-

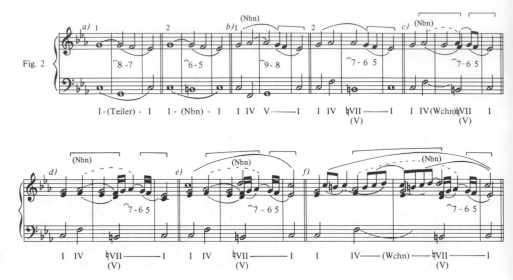

Fig. 2

7–1. Schenker, *Das Meisterwerk in der Musik*, 2, p. 60

tion progressively shorter and places them ever later in the two-measure span. By the foreground, the G and F have been reduced from whole notes covering two measures to sixteenths at the end of measure 2. The successive durational reductions are necessary only because of the arbitrary two-measure limit imposed here. A time span of two measures is indeed the length of the fugue subject being analyzed, but there is nothing systematic in Schenker's analytic approach that requires the middleground levels to contain the same number of measures as the foreground. What is to be understood by these middleground durations? If we hear the subject according to Schenker's analysis, does this mean that we somehow relate those sixteenths at the end of measure 2 to, respectively, all of measure 1 and all of measure 2? Metrically? Accentually?

A somewhat similar analytical approach appears in *Free Composition,* figure 141, in which Schenker tries several ways (including Mozart's) of incorporating the three arpeggiated thirds and the cadential motion of Mozart's variations theme from the *Piano Sonata,* K. 331, into a four-measure phrase (example 7-2).[2] Once again, the composition itself determines the durational limit of the phrase, and there is nothing essential to the analytic method that bears on or is capable of evaluating how the middleground voice leadings are to be displayed within that phrase.

7–2. Schenker, *Free Composition*, fig. 141

A second approach to rhythm is demonstrated by the analysis of a minuet by Bach, in which every level, including the background, contains specific rhythmic and metric notation. Example 7-3 illustrates the analysis up to the first double bar.[3] Schenker provides very few comments concerning this uniquely notated analysis. Other than a preference for equally long durations at the back-

7–3. Schenker, *Free Composition*, fig. 138/1

197

ground, little seems to be systematic about the choice of durations at higher levels. And because of the equal durations at the background, there is a singular lack of coordination between background events and foreground events. This is perhaps most striking in the dividing dominant of the first half of the minuet. At the foreground, the dividing dominant occurs in the final measure of the section. But at the background, the dominant is aligned with the entire second phrase. Instead of viewing the beginning of the second phrase, for instance, as a continuation of the opening tonic prolongation—or even as a durational expansion of the opening tonic prolongation—the analysis implies that the tonic that opens the second phrase is some sort of attack chord within a dominant prolongation. Such an analysis does not accord with the parallel phrase beginnings at the foreground. The problem here, as in the analyses discussed earlier, is the lack of a systematic method of determining durations and metric placements above the foreground level.

Schenker indicated, in a third approach, a possible solution to these problems in several imaginative analyses in *Free Composition* that explore the notion of expansion *(Dehnung)*.[4] The most extensive of these is an analysis of part of the slow movement of Mozart's *Symphony No. 35*[5] (see example 7-4). Schenker introduces this excerpt to show how a four- or six-measure phrase can be expanded to include more measures of music. The numbers above the measures show the position of that measure in the phrasing. Although these numbers can be interpreted as indicating a hypermeter, it is clear that meter in the traditional sense is not the issue here. (Review the discussion of examples 6-1 through 6-3.) For Schenker is not denying the continuation of the measure as a hypermetric pulse. He does not argue that measures 9–17 are only four measures long (as measures 5–8 actually are). Rather, he is demonstrating graphically the different content of measures 9–17 as opposed to measures 5–8. The D chord arriving in measure 12 is the last important structural pitch event prior to the new phrase in measure 18. As the meter keeps ticking away in measures 12–17, the music is marking time in a structural sense.

The analysis of this Mozart passage is notated on a single staff system. Neither here nor, to my knowledge, anywhere else in Schenker's published analyses, is there an analysis illustrating expansion presented along with a hierarchical analysis featuring a no-

7–4. Schenker, *Free Composition,* fig. 148/1

tated meter at each level of structure, as in example 7-1. Two of
Schenker's modes of exploration—metric notation at each level of
structure and the notion of expansion as a metric phenomenon—
have been the stimuli for several recent studies. Komar, Westergaard, and Schachter have each applied these concepts in their own
ways, to be discussed below.

In Schenker's own output, these approaches to rhythmic theory are far too limited and tentative to be considered a comprehensive approach to the subject. While Boretz and Schachter laid to rest
that rather silly criticism that Schenker's theory of tonal music ig-
nores rhythm, they and others have also acknowledged the lack of
an explicit comprehensive theory of rhythm in Schenker's work.[6]
Perhaps the surest indication of Schenker's own feelings on the subject is the lack of any assertion of his achievements in the chapter on

199

rhythm and meter in *Free Composition*. Instead of the announcements of his revolutionary achievements concerning harmony, melody, counterpoint, and form found throughout his writings, the chapter on rhythm ends by questioning the very presence of metric schemes in polyphonic music and by hesitantly exploring other subsidiary areas of musical rhythm.

RECENT THEORIES

Among recent studies that treat the relationship between hierarchical levels and rhythmic/metric phenomena are those by Yeston, Komar, Westergaard, and Schachter. Maury Yeston's 1974 dissertation, the "Stratification of Musical Rhythm,"[7] treats the interaction of different levels of rhythmic activity. But his rhythmic levels are not structural levels in the Schenkerian sense.[8] While Yeston's often perceptive comments about rhythmic motives at various levels of structure could amplify a rhythmic hierarchical analysis of the pitch structure of a piece, they are never applied in this manner in Yeston's study.[9]

Arthur Komar's 1969 dissertation, "A Theory of Suspensions,"[10] proposes a comprehensive metric theory in which every pitch at every level in a hierarchical analysis is paired with a specific duration in a specific metric position. To avoid using excessively long durations at higher levels, Komar reduces rhythmic values at middleground and background levels. Komar's approach remains the only systematic metric theory published. There are few principles for generating rhythmic values and anticipating, delaying, and otherwise altering those values. Basically, a rhythmic value at a given level can be subdivided into any number of equal time spans or any $\frac{1}{x}$ division at the next lower level. Thus, the skips of a third and a fifth in measures 1 and 2 of example 7-5 become scales at the next lower level as the passing motions are generated along with metric subdivisions. In measure 3, the whole note divides into $\frac{3}{4} + \frac{1}{4}$, implying division into quarters. Restrictions on some types of divisions prevent metric conflicts or syncopations from arising without alterations. In example 7-6, for instance, the dotted half cannot be divided directly into dotted quarters at the next lower level because that would conflict with the implied quarter-note divisions. A syncopated rhythm can rise only by an alteration of an unsyncopated rhythm, as in example 7-7. This certainly accords with our hearing

7–5

7–6

of syncopations as being in conflict with metric accentuations. Komar's simple rhythmic operations allow a wide range of applications in analyzing any tonal passage. In this sense, the approach complements Schenker's, in which passing motions, neighboring motions, octave doublings and transfers, and arpeggiations furnish the tools that can analyze all tonal music.

Although the subjects of accent and metric accent do not occupy a large portion of Komar's work, metric accent lies at the heart of his theory. A time point that is generated at a given level is metrically unaccented in relation to time points at higher levels and is metrically accented in relation to time points generated at lower levels. In example 7-8, for instance, the C in measure 1, level y, is in a

7-7

7-8

metrically unaccented position in relation to the surrounding E and
B because E and B begin at time points that arise at more background levels. At level z, the same third beat of measure 1 remains
metrically unaccented in relation to the first beats of measures 1 and
2 but is metrically accented in relation to the time points derived at
lower levels. Because all the time points in measures 1–2 of levels x,
y, and z are generated at lower levels than the downbeats of mea-

sures 1 and 3, those downbeats are metrically stronger than any in-tervening beats. According to level v, the opening downbeat of all levels in the example is the strongest metrical accent.

In virtually all tonal pieces, as the analysis moves from back-ground toward foreground, various expansions or contractions oc-cur. One metric unit may remain unchanged as preceding and fol-lowing units are expanded, creating irregular phrases and section lengths out of even units at higher levels. Or two units may be con-tracted into a single unit, creating phrase elisions. A unit may be repeated several times, creating what Komar calls a bifurcation. See measures 5–7 of Chopin's *Prelude,* op. 28, no. 1, in example 7-9. Komar considers it "undesirable to regard the D's of bars 5–6 as lower neighbors, or to regard the E's of bars 6–7 as upper neigh-

7–9. Chopin, *Prelude*, op. 28, no. 1, and analysis from Komar, *A Theory of Sus-pensions*, example 89

bors."[11] Instead, in each measure the nonharmonic tone E resolves to D as if it were the only time that happens. As noted in example 7–9, Komar analyzes measures 5–7 of Chopin's version as a thrice-repeated soprano motion that expands a six-measure phrase to eight measures at the foreground.

Example 7-10 reproduces Komar's example 100, an analysis of the slow movement of Beethoven's *Piano Sonata,* op. 13. This is the only metric analysis of a complete movement that appears in Komar's study. To allow for a compact presentation, only the bass is indicated at each level, and the more foreground levels are incom-

7–10. Komar, *A Theory of Suspensions,* example 200

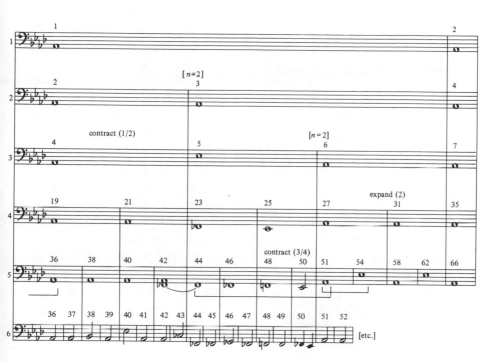

7–10. (*Continued*)

pletely sketched. The numbers above each measure are the measure
numbers at that level. By level 5, the measure numbers correspond
to those in the actual piece. The opening measure at levels 1–7 is
numbered 0 for reasons to be discussed later. The equations (such
as n = 2) indicate the number of beats added as subdivisions of the
prior level. Thus, measure 0 expands into two measures (0 and 1) at
level 2. The term "contract" indicates that part of a measure is con-
tracted as another part of that measure expands moving to the next
level. Moving from level 2 to level 3, for instance, measures 0, 1,
and 3 expand into two measures each. But measure 2 remains a single measure; hence the notation *contract* $\frac{1}{2}$, indicating that it con-
tracts to one half the size of the expansion. The barlines appear as
time points are marked off at successive levels. The barlines that extend above a given level indicate stronger metric accents than those
that begin at that level. Thus at level 4, measures 0, 8, 12, 19, 23, 27,
and 35 are strong beats, and measures 4, 10, 21, 25, and 31 are
weak beats. The result is the meter at each level of structure.

The following discussion is not so much a critique of this particular analysis as it is an exploration of this approach to tonal rhythm and meter. Komar's approach is based on the extension of meter to middleground and background levels. But it is clear that meter, as understood at the foreground, is not the issue here. Meter arises as a grouping of pulses—a grouping caused largely by harmonic changes and durational and textural accents. In most tonal music, metric relationships hold from the quickest rhythmic values up to the highest level at which the meter-creating factors operate. In this Beethoven movement, none of the meter-creating factors operates above the level of the notated meter except for a few measures at a time. Harmonic changes occur at least once a measure except in measures 8–9, 27–28, 44–45, 48–49, and 58–59.

So the measures in levels 7 and 8 are demonstrably the meter of the piece. But what about the meter at levels 1–6? How are we to understand the pulses and their grouping? Even if we grant an improbably fast tempo of ♩ = 60 for this movement, the pulses at level 5 represent eight seconds each (𝅝 = 7.5), while those at level 2 represent over a minute each (𝅝 = < 1!). Surely these are not pulses in the ordinary sense of the term.

Recall the discussion of Bach's *Prelude in A♭ Major* in chapter 3 (example 3-24). That prelude is particularly rich in true metric levels, as reflected by recordings of it that diverge in tempo by 60 percent. What is striking about these diverse performances is how the metric levels are perceived. In the slower performances, the higher metric levels do not simply move more slowly. They cease to be perceptible as meters. And in the fastest performance, in which the higher metric levels come into focus, the quickest note values and metric levels become extremely rapid spans, no longer rigorously measured notes.

I am not sure whether it is possible to specify at what point fast or slow pulses are no longer perceived in metric groupings. First, the context affects what is perceptible as meter. In the extremely slow second movement of Beethoven's *Piano Trio*, op. 70, no. 1 ("The Ghost"), for instance, many performances are as slow as ♪ = 72, making the notated $\frac{2}{4}$ meter, quite perceptible as a meter, move at ♩ = 18. Second, we, affected by very fast and very slow music written in our own century, are possibly capable of perceiving a wider range of metric pacings than our eighteenth- and nineteenth-century counterparts. But in any context there are limits to the range of meters that we can perceive simultaneously. It is doubtful, in our hypothetical ♩ = 60 performance of the "Pathétique" slow movement, that we can perceive a larger pacing of o= < 1 or even o= 7.5 as a meter. In Komar's analysis, as in any such analysis, the levels rapidly recede beyond the level at which pulses are perceptible as groupable units. Although Komar does not address this issue, it might be argued that the higher levels, taken separately, are to be understood in a considerably faster tempo than the foreground. But even if this were so, any relationship understood at a fast tempo would recede out of significance as lower levels are introduced at ever-slower tempos.

The notions of expansible time spans and even of marked changes in tempo from one level to another raise further concerns. Komar, as well as many other writers on rhythm, bases his theory on the analogy of Schenker's levels of pitch structure. But pitch and rhythm are not of the same nature, and what works well for the pitch aspects of tonality may not work as well or, indeed, may not work at all for rhythm. The crucial problem in treating rhythm like pitch is the relation between levels of structure. When a pitch configuration is analyzed by means of a simpler structure at a more background level, presumably the more background level is implied by the configuration, and the configuration is recognizable as a derivative of the more background level. A tonic at the more background level remains a prolonged tonic in the configuration; a passing motion at the more background level remains a passing motion in the configuration, even though it may be considerably elaborated. Indeed, often the principal disagreement between theorists over a given analysis is how well their differing analyses reflect such implications between levels. Such mutual implications among levels are possible because pitch events and structures retain their identity from level to level. The tonic remains the tonic, a leading tone remains a leading tone, and so forth. The foreground notes that are the representatives of a background motion are perceptibly the same as the background notes. For instance, a 3-2-1 motion at some relatively background level is elaborated extensively. The 3, the 2, and the 1 at the foreground are recognizably the representatives of those same background pitches.

But where is the analogous identity in terms of rhythmic values and metric positions? In Komar's "Pathétique" analysis, for instance, is any rhythmic aspect recognizably the same between, say, the second note at level 3 and the corresponding measure 16 at the foreground (level 8)? The Ab at level 3 is metrically weak, occurring one pulse after the opening measure 0 and one pulse before measure 2. Measure 16 is, in Komar's analysis, metrically strong, backed up by being a strong beat at four prior levels. Measure 16 is preceded by fifteen pulses, beginning with measure 1 (not measure 0), and is followed by seven pulses before measure 23 (the equivalent of measure 2 at Komar's level 3). So, in terms of duration, metric position, and relative position before and after corresponding points, measure 16 at the foreground differs from measure 1 at level 3.

Theorists other than Komar have differed on how far toward the background it is profitable to pursue metric analysis. Schachter's durational reductions[12] retain a metric structure only up to "that level of the middleground where the form of the piece first becomes apparent."[13] Schachter argues that to continue durational or metric notation above that level would only indicate the pacing of the structural progression in terms of a "basic duration. . . . But to do so would be misleading, for the basic duration takes on meaning only in relation to the groupings of bars and to the form." The level to which Schachter asserts the existence of a metric structure is, as in Komar's analysis, a few levels above the primary metric level. Westergaard is more cautious than Komar or Schachter, retaining specific durations to show pacing up to the level of phrases, but dropping a meter signature and metric implications above the primary metric level.[14]

Metric Analysis at the Phrase Level. A crucial factor determining a theorist's attitude toward metric structure above the primary metric level is his or her treatment of cadences. If we move from background toward foreground, the first essential harmony of a phrase and the cadence harmony are generally the first and second events in the phrase to appear. Komar, for whom prior appearance implies metric accent, therefore places a metric accent on the cadential measures 4 and 8 in the opening period of the slow movement of the "Pathétique" (review example 7-10). It is because of the strong cadences and the desire for a regular alternation of strong and weak measures that Komar then postulates measure 0. With measure 0, the opening tonic of the piece can be strong at all higher levels but weak at the foreground. In the opening period of this Beethoven slow movement, the cadential measures of the antecedent and consequent phrases are followed by a continuation of the same harmony. The repeat of the opening period in measures 9–16 begins with a continuation of the cadential tonic from measure 8, an argument used by Komar to support his contention of a metrically weak phrase beginning.[15]

Westergaard treats phrase structure somewhat differently. He considers the first and last measures of most phrases metrically accented, calling them primary beats. A number of secondary downbeats intervene between these primary beats, giving rise to the number of measures in that phrase. His principal reason for rejecting metric regularity in favor of primary beats at the beginnings and endings of phrases and secondary beats in the middles is one that we have already discussed in chapter 6—the reason that phrases mark off separate spans of time (or musical thoughts) and do not simply flow into one another as beats in consecutive measures do. Example 7-11 illustrates Westergaard's approach. Note that metric notation is maintained only up to the primary metric level. At the level labeled "measures," there is no meter signature. The beginning and ending measures of each phrase are set off by the barlines indicating the primary beats. At the level labeled "phrases," durations indicate pacing, but no longer carry metric significance. Westergaard, thus, is in agreement with Cone's view of phrase structure—that phrases begin and end with metric accents.[16]

The other alternative is to accept phrase beginnings as metrically accented and most cadences as metrically weak. This approach denies any direct relation between the level at which a pitch or harmony arises and its accentual status. This is Schenker's position and also the one adopted by Schachter in his durational analyses. Schachter recognizes metrically strong cadences when the cadential arrival elides with the beginning of a new section, as at the beginning of the codetta (measure 51) of the allegretto movement of Beethoven's *Piano Sonata*, op. 14, no. 1.[17] But in general he opts for cadences that are on the last beat of a hypermeasure.

In addition to his general assertion that cadences are inherently unaccented, Schachter's commentaries include two discussions of the metric status of cadences. In support of a metrically weak final tonic arrival in Chopin's *Prelude*, op. 28, no. 3, Schachter cites only that "the goal tonic of the soprano [measure 26] falls at the end of a legato slur—a notation that suggests that it is rhythmically, as well as metrically, weak."[18] Yet Chopin's slurs also cross the arrival on the dominant in measure 24, a dominant that is metrically strong at every level in Schachter's analysis (see example 7-

7–11. Westergaard, *An Introduction to Tonal Theory*, fold-out example at the end

7–11. *(Continued)*

7–11. *(Continued)*

12). The other discussion of the metric status of a cadence concerns the tonic arrival at the beginning of the second-movement codetta in Beethoven's *Piano Sonata*, op. 14, no. 1. Schachter's analysis allows a strong arrival on measure 51 because of an expansion of the preceding phrase by the extension of the subdominant harmony. He writes that "it is very constructive to compare the rhythmic effect of the final tonic, which falls on a true 'downbeat,' with that of the tonic that closes the first A section on a metrically weak bar (bar 16). Yet this significant difference would be minimized (or even ignored altogether) by an approach that in principle regards cadential tonics as 'downbeat,' no matter what the actual metrics might be."[19] But measures 51 and 16 are not potential equivalents. The primary metric level of this movement is two notated measures, established by durational and textural accents, and occasionally by

7–12. Schacter, "Durational Reduction," example 4

the harmonic rhythm. All even-numbered measures (including measure 16) are metrically weak.[20]

SUMMARY

Applying rhythm and meter to linear analysis illustrates a given theorist's attitudes toward crucial issues more than it leads to a solution of those issues. Cone, who does not apply specific rhythms to hierarchical pitch analyses, agrees with Westergaard concerning the metric structure of phrases. Schachter and Komar agree in the extension of metric notation far above the level of the primary meter, in the conceptual regularity of meter at higher levels, and in expansions and other alterations of time spans to allow the transformation of regular meters at higher levels of structure to the irregular phrase and section lengths so characteristic of the surface of tonal music. They even agree, along with Westergaard, that the opening and closing harmonies of a phrase are the first to appear in the middleground. Yet Schachter, Komar, and Westergaard hold completely opposing positions on the metric nature of phrases.

It is for this reason that in the present book, the chapter on rhythm and linear analysis follows discussions of accent, meter, hypermeter, and phrasing. Allen Forte closed his 1959 introductory article on Schenker[21] by listing five crucial unsolved problems in music theory and suggested some ways in which Schenker's ideas could contribute toward a solution. The first problem mentioned is constructing a theory of rhythm for tonal music. Forte quotes paragraph 21 from *Free Composition,* rendered here in Ernst Oster's translation.

Rhythm can no more exist in the fundamental structure than it can in a strict-counterpoint *cantus firmus* exercise.

Only when, through voice-leading transformations, linear progressions arise in the upper and lower voices of the middleground, does a rhythmic ordering issue from the necessity of counterpointing the voices against each other. All rhythm in music comes from counterpoint and only from counterpoint. . . .

In the middleground every individual level has its own specific rhythm, according to the extent of its contrapuntal content. Thus rhythm, too, progresses through various transformational stages until it reaches the foreground, just as do meter and form, which also represent end-results of a progressive contrapuntal differentiation. . . .

Forte then poses two questions: "At what structural level do rhythmic events begin to determine the tonal structure of a given work?" and "What is the nature of the relationship between the constituent rhythmic levels in a given work?"[22] Answers to these and similar questions may already reside in the points of agreement among theorists who have written on the subject and among musicians in general. Concerning rhythm at the background level, for instance, all theorists, with the nominal exception of Komar, agree with Schenker's assertion that the fundamental structure is arhythmic. And as we have seen, Komar's meter at relatively background levels is not what is ordinarily meant by meter at the foreground.

Schachter asserts that the pacing of events becomes important at the level at which the form of the piece first appears. In connection with Schubert's *Valse Sentimentale,* op. 50, no. 13, he demonstrates by means of example 7-13 how little is gained by merely laying out the fundamental or background structure in a metric scheme. Only at the middleground level that illustrates the form does the use of durations begin to relate to events in the particular piece (example 7-14). On this point, Schachter is in agreement with

7–13. Schachter, "Durational Reduction," example 14

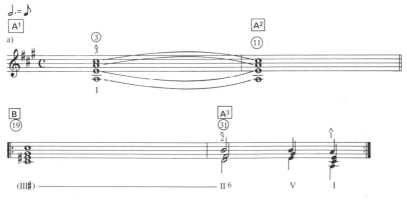

7–14. Schachter, "Durational Reduction," example 12

215

Westergaard's analyses, and, indeed, with traditional theorists of musical form. For meter is not the issue here—the durations show only the pacing and proportions of formal divisions in the piece.

Rhythmic interaction at lower levels gets more and more specific. Larger formal sections subdivide into phrases. And below the phrase level, the actual measures of the piece appear.

All theorists agree that the background is ametric in the sense that we understand meter at the foreground. All theorists agree that shortly below the level of the fundamental structure, the pacing and proportions of formal divisions in the piece come into play. Subdivisions of larger sections give the phrase lengths, with or without extensions, contractions, and other alterations. Finally, all theorists agree that up to the measure level (or the primary metric level when that is higher or lower than the level of the notated measure), meter functions. It is between the measure level and the phrase level that disagreements arise between those who would assert metric relationships (Schachter, Berry, Komar) and those who do not recognize meter much above the primary metric level. So the disagreement, in Cone's terms, concerns primarily the level at which "meter . . . must yield to a more organic rhythmic principle."[23]

As discussed in chapter 6 of the present work, the preference for or against metric structuring for one or more levels above the primary metric level is a matter of interpretation, not a provable position. This preference reflects different attitudes toward continuity. Linear analysis, as shown in this chapter, does not provide any decisive proofs for or against either position. Rather, a given theorist's linear analyses will reflect that theorist's attitudes to the extent that he or she wishes to incorporate metric notations in those analyses. The same is true of other rhythmic issues, whether they be the definition of accent or the role of rhythmic continuity and motives. The application of linear analysis per se will not lead directly to a solution of these issues.

Linear analysis is a powerful analytical method for tonal music, revealing, in addition to the obvious pitch and motivic structures, a great deal of information about the rhythms of a piece: the ordering of events, the relationships among events at the same levels and between different levels of structure (local and long-range events), patterns of repetition (motivic structure), the placement of goals and/or motions leading to those goals on many levels of structure, and so forth. These facets are displayed whether or not the analysis utilizes specific rhythmic and metric notations at some or all levels. In that the incorporation of rhythmic and metric notations raises the problems cited in this chapter and in that rhythmic processes both at the foreground and at higher levels involve far more complex matters than merely the assignment of a duration and metric position, it may well be that traditional methods of notating hierarchic analyses are as well or better suited to reveal rhythm than more metrically notated analyses. The varieties of accentuation (discussed in chapter 2), the relations between accentuations and meter up to the primary metric level (discussed in chapters 3 and 4), the continuities, multiple goals, pacings, and accentuations that interact above the primary metric level (discussed in chapters 5, 6, 8, and 9, as well as in this chapter) do not lend themselves to the notation of hierarchical linear analyses.

8

RHYTHM AND FORM

The study of musical form commonly considers several aspects of rhythm: primarily proportions among the sections of a piece and the rhythmic differentiation of different sections in a piece. This study has already discussed the second of these issues. Sectional proportions as an aspect of form bear on both the individuality of a given piece as well as on stylistic and historical developments. Consider as a single example the first movement of Beethoven's "Eroica" *Symphony*. Knowing that the development section and coda added together make up slightly more than half the length of the movement (a bit less than half if the exposition is repeated) makes clear the relatively long expanses of time in the development and coda for the wide-ranging harmonic, tonal, thematic, and textural drama of this movement. And comparing these proportions to earlier large sonata-form movements dramatizes the new musical horizons Beethoven explored. The first movement of Mozart's *String Quintet in C*, K. 515, for instance, is close to the duration of the "Eroica's" first movement in terms of time. In the Mozart, there is no coda, and the development is only one sixth of the movement (one ninth if the exposition is repeated). In contrast to the "Eroica," the bulk of the Mozart movement consists of the more formally structured exposition and recapitulation.

There is another aspect of rhythm in form that has received very little attention. This is the relationship between a passage's rhythmic continuity (including phrasing) and both the type of form of a movement and the placement of the passage within that form. This subject is the focus of the present chapter.

Different types of formal layouts promote different types of phrasing patterns, cadences, composite rhythms, and so forth.[1] All tonal music includes cadences, texture changes, new themes, new

tonal areas, and other such factors that close off sections and separate them from one another. Counterbalancing these are other factors that promote continuity across sectional divisions—factors
such as phrasing elisions that link the end of one section to the beginning of the next, gradual instead of abrupt textural and rhythmic
changes, and processes that continue through several sections (continuity in tempo, theme, composite rhythm, dynamics, and so
forth). A fundamental distinction exists between those sectional
forms and contexts that promote closed sections set off from one
another and those forms and sections (especially sonata form) that
promote continuity.

SECTIONAL FORMS

Variation Forms

Sets of variations generally feature a number of short sections set off
from each other by conclusive cadences and pauses. Each new variation often contains its own motives, its own rhythms, and, sometimes, its own tempo. The themes for late eighteenth- and
nineteenth-century sets of variations are most often in simple binary or rounded binary form with each part ending in a clear-cut
cadence. The variations generally follow the structure of the theme.

To create continuities larger than the single variations, composers often grouped the early variations in a cycle by accelerations
or decelerations in the composite rhythm over several variations.
The finale of Mozart's *Piano Sonata in D,* K. 284, the first movement of Beethoven's *Piano Sonata in Ab*, op. 26, and the finale of
Brahms' *Symphony No. 4* each feature an accelerating composite
rhythm in the early variations. The first five of Mozart's variations
on *"Ah vous dirais-je, Maman,"* K. 265, feature a decelerating
composite rhythm. The theme is in quarter notes. The first five variations decelerate from continuous sixteenths (variations 1 and 2) to
continuous eighth-triplets (variations 3 and 4) to eighths and then
eighths with pairs of sixteenths (variation 5).

Several Beethoven variation movements add imaginative
touches to such composite-rhythm schemes. In the slow movement
of the *String Quartet,* op. 18, no. 5, the theme offers mostly quarters and eighths. The first variation features continuous sixteenths,
the second variation continuous sixteenth-triplets, and the third

variation continuous thirty-seconds. Yet against this acceleration, the overall effect of these variations is a deceleration of activity because of texture and articulation. The ensemble staccato sixteenths and fugal texture of variation 1, with syncopated sforzandos at the cadences, give way to the homophony and regular accompanimental rhythms of variation 2. The thirty-seconds in the third variation are an accompanimental pattern to the quarters and eighths of the melodic fragments derived from the theme. Most thirty-seconds are step-related, and all are under slurs. Only three instruments play at a time, except at the cadences. The resulting deceleration process against the apparent acceleration in these three variations prepares for the revelatory chorale-style chromatic harmonization in quarters and eighths in variation 4, a variation that combines the slowest durations and the most uniform texture of the movement with the fastest and most distantly related harmonic changes.

A similar process, though with quite a different effect, begins the set of variations in the finale of the *"Eroica" Symphony*. After the bombastic fanfare leads to the extremely simple pizzicato theme, the first three variations accelerate from eighths through eighth-triplets to sixteenths. The faster values proceed from imitative motives in variation 1 to imitation becoming accompaniment in variation 2 to accompanimental sixteenths in variation 3 as the principal melody of the movement enters. As in the quartet variations just discussed, the acceleration is partly an illusion—the sixteenths are accompanied by a change to a homophonic texture and a more broadly phrased melody.

Rhythmic processes such as these can link several variations but cannot overcome the ultimate sectional nature of sets of variations. The great variation cycles that maintain discrete variations—Bach's *Goldberg Variations*, Beethoven's *Diabelli Variations*, the variation sets in Beethoven's late piano sonatas and quartets, Brahms' *Variations on a Theme by Haydn*, op. 56, and so forth—create their effect by the marvelous inventiveness of the individual variations, the variety displayed by the variations following one another in time, and the structures created by the juxtaposition of large blocks of material. The more fluid dramatic sweep and the single overarching shape of sonata-form movements is alien to variation sets. The difference in conception between these forms is perhaps most obvious at the ends of variation sets. Think of the finale of Beethoven's *Piano Sonata*, op. 109, or the return of the aria at the end of the *Goldberg Variations*. The ecstatic contemplation of the entire unadorned, returned themes that end these cycles would be inconceivable in a sonata-form movement or a more through-composed Baroque form.

Another approach to variation movements was explored by Beethoven in the slow movement of the *Fifth Symphony* and the finales of the *Third* and *Ninth* symphonies. Strict variations occur alongside of developmental sections more characteristic of other forms. In these movements, rhythmic continuities characteristic of forms other than variations predominate.

Passacaglia or ground-bass variations allow different compositional options in terms of continuity because the separate variations need not be set off from one another. Some compositions, such as Bach's *Passacaglia in C Minor*, BWV 582, retain a clear-cut cadence and distinct texture change at the end of each variation. Accelerations in the composite rhythm from variation to variation and greater or lesser textural changes set off larger sections of the *Passacaglia* from one another. In the chaconne of Bach's *Partita No. 1 for Violin Alone* (BWV 1004), many variations flow into the next variation because of the lack of any textural changes or clear-cut cadential articulations. This is especially true in the variations with faster note values and the arpeggiando variations. Pairing of variations, as at the very opening, creates a quasi-periodic structure in several sections.[2]

The finale of Brahms' *Symphony No. 4* displays a remarkable range of continuities within the strict limitations of the recurring eight-measure passacaglia theme. The movement divides into four sections of uneven length (akin to A B A' plus developmental coda) on the basis of meter and tempo changes as well as the reprises of earlier variations in the third section.

measures 1–96 in $\frac{3}{4}$ = variations 1–12 (A)
measures 97–128 in $\frac{3}{2}$ = variations 13–16 (B)
measures 129–252 in $\frac{3}{4}$ = variations 17–31 (A')
measures 253–311 in $\frac{3}{4}$ at più allegro are the coda

The first section features a continual acceleration in composite rhythm through variation 10. A relaxation in variations 11 and 12 leads to the doubled measure length in the second section. The increasing rhythmic activity in variations 1–10 occurs as the varia-

221

tions group into shorter sectional subdivisions. The pairing of increasingly active rhythms with ever-shorter sectional subdivisions creates the heightened drama as the opening section proceeds. The opening section, then, is structured as follows:

section number	contents	predominant value in composite rhythm
1	theme (mm. 1–8)	𝅗𝅥.
2–5	four variations (mm. 9–40). Ends with cadence.	♩ 𝅗𝅥, then ♩'s, then some ♪'s.
6–8	three variations (mm. 41–64). Ends with cadence.	♪'s and ♪ (3), then ♪. 𝅘𝅥𝅯
9–10	two variations (mm. 65–80)	𝅘𝅥𝅯's, then 𝅘𝅥𝅯 (6)'s and 𝅘𝅥𝅯's

shorter sections ↓   faster values ↓

Brahms makes use of the repeated E that links the end and beginning of each statement of the passacaglia theme to shape the continuities between variations. When the change of harmony supporting these E's is from tonic to nontonic (subdominant or submediant) and there is no overlapping of material between variations, the end of one variation is completely set off from the beginning of the next, as in measures 8–9 (variations 1–2). Variations 2–5 all flow into one another for a variety of reasons. Both harmony and phrasing contribute to the connection of variations 2 and 3 (measures 16–17). The French sixth in measure 15 progresses to E major in measure 16, sounding like a French sixth proceeding to V, resolving on the A major chord that begins variation 3 in measure 17. The entrance of the woodwind melody during measure 16 contributes to the continuity. Variations 3 and 4 are linked by the melodic nonharmonic tones that preclude any cessation of motion in measure 24. The fourth and fifth variations are linked by the appoggiatura harmony ("IV^6_4") on the tonic arrival in measure 32—a harmony that does not resolve to the tonic until measure 33 begins variation 5. Variation 5 concludes with the first true cadence thus far. The hemiola over the dominant in measures 38–39 strengthens the hypermetric accent on the cadential arrival—an accent reinforced by the crescendo leading to measure 40. For the first time since measures 8–9, there is a clear break between variations 5 and 6.

Other continuities link variations 6–8. The tonic harmony maintained across measures 48–49 (variations 6–7) is reinforced by the direct pitch repetition in the upper strings and the retention of the eighth-versus-triplet texture. The introduction of more than one harmony per measure at the end of variation 7 (measures 54–55) prepares for the extra dominant in measure 56 that resolves on the beginning of measure 58 (variation 8). The cadence that ends variation 8 recalls the cadence ending variation 5 (measures 38–40) with the hemiola preparation, the identical melodic pitches, and the cadential appoggiatura.

Neither variation 9 nor variation 10 ends with a cadence (measures 65–72, 73–80). But their parallel structures and the degree to which variation 11 begins in a new manner (measure 81) set off variations 9 and 10 as a single unit. Later sections feature only a few cadences, none of which is strongly articulated until the coda. The connections between variations are accomplished in ever-changing ways.

A rather different approach to continuity that supersedes the variational divisions is found in the ground-bass aria *Oh! Belinda* from Purcell's *Dido and Aeneas*. The opening section in C appears in example 8-1. There are eleven repetitions of the four-measure ground. Only twice (in measures 9–12 and 25–28) does a division in the melodic part coincide with both the beginning and ending of any repetition of the bass. The first eight measures join to make a single unit. Measures 9–16 seem to be an answering eight-measure phrase until the melody in measure 16 spills over into measure 17 (depicting Dido's "not-to-be-confest" torment bursting forth?). Measures 17–33 repeat measures 1–17. But because of the melodic ending in measure 17, the recurrence of the opening phrase sounds as if it were aligned differently than on its first appearance, even though the music is identical. Most remarkable is the later shift in phrasing that sets "Peace and I are strangers grown." Measures 36–39 function as the first four-measure phrase in a 4 + 5 parallel period that is totally out of alignment with the repetition pattern of the ground bass. The setting allows for a double word painting. First, there is the misalignment of the melodic phrases and the bass repetition, reflecting the gulf between "peace and I." Second, the words

8–1. Purcell, *Dido and Aeneas*, no. 2

"peace and I" fall on the two measures of tonic harmony; they "are strangers grown" as the harmony moves.

This type of variation writing creates over the strict bass divisions the phrasing disparities between voices characteristic of contrapuntal styles. Chapter 9 explores such phrasing and rhythmic situations in greater depth.

Ternary and Rondo Forms

Movements in ternary form (ABA) and some types of rondos are like variations in that the movement as a whole is put together from discrete sections. From a rhythmic perspective, ternary forms differ from variations primarily in that the contrasting sections differ from one another in structure.

Minuet-and-trio and scherzo-and-trio movements are almost exclusively in ternary form. Exceptions are generally modeled on ternary form. In the scherzo of Beethoven's *Symphony No. 7*, for instance, the trio returns a second time followed by another statement of the scherzo: scherzo-trio-scherzo-trio-scherzo. Occasional movements contain more than one trio, such as the final movement of Bach's *Brandenburg Concerto No. 1* (with three trios) or the scherzo of Schumann's *Piano Quintet,* op. 44 (with two trios). These movements are, in effect, rondos.

Occasional movements contain transitions between the minuet (or scherzo) and the trio, or between the trio and the return to the opening. (See the minuet of Haydn's *Symphony No. 104* for an instance of the latter.) And occasional movements add a codetta to round off the movement. (See the scherzo to Beethoven's *Seventh Symphony.*) The essence of the form, however, is in the alternation of separate, closed sections, each complete in itself. This is true whether the ternary form consists of separate dances (or stylized dances) or of the sections of a more continuous movement.

Within multimovement works, continuous ternary form is most common in slow movements. The outer sections of most movements in this form share many structural characteristics. By the nature of the form, these outer sections begin and end in the tonic key. They invariably contain a simple phrasing pattern, almost always with no phrasing extensions. The first section almost always ends with a single arrival on the tonic. (A reiterated tonic cadence ending the first section would create too great a sense of finality.)

The nine slow movements of Haydn's string quartets that are

in ternary form all follow this pattern (op. 54, no. 3; 64, no. 3; 64, no. 4; 64, no. 5; 64, no. 6; 71, no. 1; 74, no. 3; 76, no. 2, and 103). The A sections are generally rounded binary in construction, usually with both sections repeated, either literally or with varied figuration: a :‖:b a′ :‖ . The slow movement of op. 74, no. 3 "The Riders"), presented in example 8-2, is representative of this form. A single ten-measure phrase (2 + 2 + 6) and its repeat form the opening section. The phrase modulates to and cadences in the dominant. The b section after the double bar lasts four measures, transforming the dominant from I in its own key to V in the tonic key. An eight-measure phrase (2 + 2 + 4) begins like the opening phrase, but remains in and cadences in the tonic key. The cadence is similar to, though not a literal transposition of, the cadence in V that ends the first phrase. The A′ section retains the structure of the opening section without repeats. There are numerous changes of figuration, especially in the first-violin part. After the conclusion of the return, there is a five-measure coda that reiterates a cadence on I.

This formal outline is pretty much the same in all the ternary-form slow movements, whether the middle section is developmental or simply a contrasting theme. The final section of the movement is often extended by a tonic pedal, a few cadences, one after another, or a deceptive resolution of the final dominant leading to a more emphatic tonic cadence. The extent to which these movements are similar to variation movements is evidenced by those variation slow movements by Haydn that alternate two themes, such as the slow movement that opens Haydn's *String Quartet*, Op. 55, no. 2. Continuous ternary form, not unlike Classical theme-and-variations, is essentially a contemplative one, featuring closed sections.

This is true even if the dimensions of the form are expanded, as in the slow movement of Haydn's *Symphony No. 104*. There, the rounded binary structure of the opening is extended to thirty-seven measures.

a	b		a′
(4 + 4) parallel per-:‖‖:iod cadencing in V.	8 measures ending on V	(4 + opening phrase returns	12 eliding to 5) considerably expanded consequent phrase ending in a five-measure tonic pedal

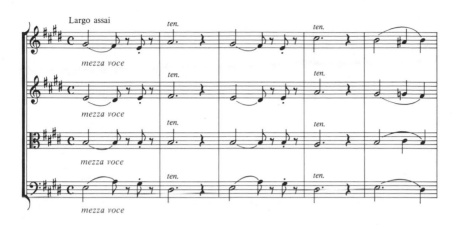

8–2. Haydn, *String Quartet*, op. 74, no. 3, second movement

8–2. *(Continued)*

There is still only a single arrival on the tonic that is extended from measures 33 to 37. In the final section of the movement (measures 74ff.), the first part (a) recurs with only minor orchestrational changes (mm. 74–81). Its written-out repeat (mm. 82–89) is considerably varied in figuration but retains the same phrasing and harmonic structure. The b part also returns with new figuration (mm. 90–97), as does the opening phrase of a (mm. 98–101). What was the twelve-measure phrase is now considerably extended to twenty measures (mm. 102–21) leading back to the opening of a′ (mm. 122–25). This second time, the twelve measures are extended to fifteen (mm. 126–40) and the final tonic pedal is extended to twelve measures. But the simple form remains clear-cut, and there is still a single arrival on the tonic at the end.

The same types of phrasing patterns occur in later ternary-form movements. See the slow movement of Beethoven's *String Quartet,* op. 18, no. 2, the slow movement of his *Piano Sonata,* op. 79, the slow movement of Schubert's *Piano Sonata in B♭,* op. post., or the *Poco allegretto* movement of Brahms' *Symphony No. 3* for four instances.

SONATA FORM

Sonata form differs in nature from these sectional forms. The essence of sonata form is a single overarching tonal motion that begins at the opening and comes to its conclusion at the end of the movement. Each passage in a sonata-form movement has its own role to play in the overall form and, therefore, its own internal structure. The themes that announce each of the key areas in the exposition, for instance, are more often than not presented in discrete phrases, as opposed to transitional, conclusive, or developmental passages that feature more continuous music and eliding phrases.

Few generalizations can be made about the structure of most passages in sonata-form movements. First theme groups occur in a wide range of phrasing organizations. Transition sections hardly exist in some movements but are extensive in others. Development sections and codas are different in every movement. But there is one section of most Classical sonata-form movements that possesses a common phrasing structure—the second theme group. This structure arises from the fact that second theme groups must perform two potentially contradictory roles in every sonata-form movement. They must establish the new key area, yet must hold off a conclusive arrival on the tonic of the new key as long as possible. For when the second theme group recurs in the recapitulation, it generally follows music in the tonic key (the first theme group). Premature closure would make the remainder of the recapitulation sound like a perfunctory tag.

In order to fulfill these roles, second theme groups, whatever their length or the number of themes, tend to begin with phrases or a period with extensions or elisions delaying the cadence of the consequent phrase. Later in the second theme group is usually a series of ever-shorter cadential phrases, each eliding with the next. The opening phrases establish the new key without necessarily cadencing in it conclusively; the later elisions and reiterated cadences project the finality of the section but hold off the final resolution until the end.

The first-movement exposition of Beethoven's *Piano Sonata,* op. 14, no. 2, provides a case in point (example 8-3). The second theme group opens with an eight-measure period (measures 26–33). The authentic cadence that would have ended the consequent phrase in measure 33 elides with the beginning of another period. Again the consequent is four measures long and ends with a half cadence (measures 33–36). The consequent phrase is extended by a tonicized subdominant to nine measures (measures 37–45). Once again, the authentic cadence elides with a new phrase (in measure 45). This time, the phrase is much shorter and consists entirely of the cadential portion of the previous phrase. This new cadence in measure 47 elides with the beginning of yet another phrase group. This phrase group is occupied largely with a series of deceptively resolving dominants. The last dominant emphatically resolves to the tonic in measure 58. The ensuing tonic pedal features ever-faster dominant-tonic progressions.

Composite rhythm joins registral, thematic, and voice-leading factors to support the structural drive of this section. The steady sixteenths of measures 26–40 become the thirty-seconds of measures 41–43 and 45, leading to the two cadential arrivals in measures 44–45 and 46–47. The rising register in measures 33–43 complements the increasingly active composite rhythm to help project the shape of the period. (If Beethoven's piano had exceeded high F, measure 43 would surely have gone up to F♯, just as the corresponding measure in the recapitulation ascends to B ♮.) Registral changes in the melody take less and less time as the section progresses. In measures 26–32, the melody progresses by only a second or third during any beat. In measures 33–36, the span increases to a fourth. The ascending skip of a sixth in measure 39 achieves the highest note thus far in the piece but leads to a repeated note. The thirty-seconds in measures 41–43 remain in a narrow range until the octave scale at the end of measure 43. The span of a twelfth in a beat and a half in measure 45 is unprecedented here. In the low registers, the low A to D in measures 57–58 leads to the final tonic pedal, returning for the first time to the bass register of measures 26 and 29.

8–3. Beethoven, *Piano Sonata*, op. 14, no. 2, first movement

8–3. *(Continued)*

Many sonata-form expositions return to their opening motives to conclude the second theme group in what is sometimes
called a closing theme or closing group. In this movement, the reference to the opening is a subtle one (see example 8-4). As here, the
motivic reference is usually cast in short, repetitive phrasing units,
reinforcing the final cadences.

The resulting structure of this second theme group projects a
drama and a dynamism not found in the sectional forms discussed

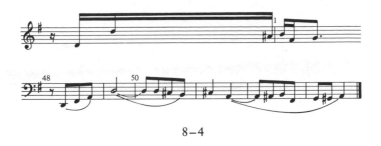

8–4

earlier in this chapter. The essence of sonata form is not to be found in thematic contrast, for thematic contrasts can occur in most any form. Haydn has surely demonstrated that a single theme can suffice for a sonata-form movement. And it is not merely a single overarching key scheme for a movement that defines sonata form. It is the rhythmic drama—an amalgam of phrasing and all the aspects of pacing—that is mandated by the special requirements of the second theme group. Even the predominance of a more lyrical "second theme" can be traced to this rhythmic structuring. For the periodic phrasing and key establishment that work so well at the opening of the second them group point toward a lyrical theme presented in balanced phrases.

The rhythmic-rhetorical shape noted in this Beethoven second theme group occurs in relatively terse movements as well as in extended ones. In the first movement of Mozart's *Piano Sonata*, K. 545, for instance, the entire second theme group lasts only fifteen measures and is cast as a single period with extensions (see example 8-5).

The repeated phrase division in measures 14–17 serves as an antecedent, establishing the new key and presenting, by virtue of the repetition, a point of stasis. The four-measure harmonic sequence, the two-measure supertonic, and one measure each on the cadential $\frac{6}{4}$ and the dominant lead with ever-greater urgency to the conclusive cadence that ends the section. The cadence in measure 26 elides with a one-measure closing phrase, itself elided into its repetition. As in many second theme groups, especially in concertos, the trill in measure 25 is the apex of an acceleration in the composite rhythm immediately before the cadential arrival.

By contrast, the second theme group in the first movement of Mozart's *String Quintet in C*, K. 515, is fifty-eight measures long

8–5. Mozart, *Piano Sonata*, K. 545, first movement

(mm. 86–143) in a 143-measure exposition. It opens with an antecedent phrase eight measures long (2 + 2 + 4), ending with a half cadence (86–93). The second phrase begins in parallel fashion, with a new melody joining the earlier figuration. But after its fifth measure, the phrase begins harmonic and melodic sequences that delay the arrival on the dominant until the fourteenth measure of the phrase (107). The cadential-$^6_4$-to-dominant progression occupies two measures, eliding first into a literal repetition and then into a five-measure-long conclusive ending. In all, then, the consequent phrase totals twenty-two measures. The cadence of this period in measure 115 elides with the beginning of a new pair of phrases. This time, the antecedent is only five measures long, made up of one-measure motivic subdivisions. The cadence is on the tonic, eliding with the consequent phrase. Once again, the consequent is considerably longer, thirteen measures in all. It, too, ends with a cadence that elides with a repetition of the cadence. The conclusive arrival on I in measure 131 initiates a tonic pedal that lasts for the remainder of the exposition. This closing section begins with a new melody derived from the first-violin motive at the beginning of the movement. Over the pedal are affirmations of the tonic at ever-shorter intervals of time.

In works from Beethoven's middle period, a greater diversity of material and moods is incorporated into second theme groups. Yet the basic structural layout is the same as that of the movements we have surveyed. Consider the first movement of the "Appassionata" *Sonata,* op. 57. The second theme group is short in terms of measures (thirty-one measures) but covers a scope not found in the earlier movements we have discussed. The opening section is a parallel period with no conclusion to the consequent phrase. The first phrase (measures 36–39) ends with an imperfect cadence. The second phrase simply evaporates over the dominant until the tonic arrival that finally occurs in measure 51 is in no sense a cadence to the first phrase. The next section, beginning in measure 51, is again a parallel period with an extended cadence to the consequent phrase. The extension this time is short—the antecedent phrase reaches the cadential dominant in its fourth measure, the consequent phrase lands on the tonic in its seventh measure. A series of repeated one-measure cadential phrases follows, with each phrase eliding into the next.

Despite its length in terms of time and number of measures, this movement is remarkable for its tautness throughout. Sections connect to each other almost seamlessly without ending conclusively. The opening F-minor material slips into the dominant of A♭ by a simple change in a recurring phrase in measure 23. The rhythmic momentum of the transition section becomes accompaniment at the beginning of the second theme group. The conclusion of the exposition connects seamlessly with the beginning of the development. The repeated bass eighths that continue from the end of the development into the first theme group in the recapitulation prevent a tonic resolution as the opening theme returns. The end of the recapitulation leads directly into the coda. As a result, the più allegro (mm. 239ff.) that concludes the movement contains a fuller version of the type of concluding phrases than appeared at the end of either the exposition or the recapitulation: a series of ever-shorter cadential phrases, each eliding with the beginning of the next. Part of the extraordinary energy of these final measures arises from the absence of any such concluding passages earlier in the movement. The genius of this movement, as well as of so many other extended middle-Beethoven movements, is that the expanded dimensions of the movement (in relation to earlier sonata forms) lead to a more compact sense of a single overarching structure—not to a relaxation of the unity and continuity of the whole.

Many, if not most, nineteenth-century composers who adopted the larger dimensions of Beethoven's sonata forms did not also re-create the single overarching structure of the movement as a whole. The dimensions of each individual section of a movement were expanded until those sections began to take on a form of their own. The whole movement sometimes seems like a series of separate pieces strung together. Such a construction appears already in many compositions of Schubert. In the first movement of the *Piano Sonata in B♭*, op. post., the first theme group is a complete ternary form. Only the final tonic in measure 45 is absent. In the finale, a sonata-rondo movement, the first theme group itself is a seventy-three-measure, five part rondo (A B^1 A B^2 A). After a brief and obvious transition, the second theme group begins with a miniature sonata form (see example 8–6).

measures	section	
86–95	first theme group in F major	
96–103	transition modulating to . . .	"exposition"
104–19	second theme group in D major	
120–29	"development"-retransition to . . .	"development"

130–37	first theme group in F major	⎫	
138–53	second theme group in F major	⎬	"recapitulation"
		⎭	

These small forms creating closed sections are antithetical to the progressive structures of earlier sonata-form movements.

In the first movement of Schumann's *Symphony No. 3* ("The Rhenish"), op. 97, the first theme group is in a ternary structure common to many nineteenth-century sonata forms: A, an opening theme (measures 1–24); B, a contrasting section using motives of the opening theme or a secondary theme, less defined than the first (25–56); A', a triumphant return to the opening theme (57–73). The second theme group is a large binary construction, each half beginning with "the second theme" proper (mm. 95-126, 127-65). A series of cadential phrases ends the section (mm. 165–84).

In many sonata-form movements written later in the nineteenth century, the different sections become even more disparate from each other. The first movement of Liszt's *Faust Symphony* is an extreme instance. The individual sections are in different tempos and are widely separated from each other in a sprawling, episodic structure. In the first movement of Mahler's *Symphony No. 4*, the exposition concludes with a return to the first theme group material in the tonic, truly making a closed section out of the open-ended tonal structure of sonata-form expositions.

In Tchaikovsky's music, the separate theme groups are often in different tempos. But in some movements, the change in tempo is only a change in metric level. Review the discussion of the *Romeo and Juliet Fantasy-Overture* in chapter 4. In this composition, the first theme group in the exposition is a ternary form (measures 111–20, 121–49, 150–60); the second theme group presents blocks of musical material in a five-part rondo-plus-coda layout (A, mm. 183–91; B, 192–211; A, 212–19; C, 220–33; A, 234–42; coda, 242–71). What distinguishes a piece like *Romeo and Juliet* from similar long and sectionalized Schubert movements is the recapitulation. The entire section is recast. Only twelve measures of the first theme group recur—just a single statement of the principal theme (mm. 352–63). After the briefest of transitions, the components of the second theme group recur in a new ordering, much connecting material is omitted, and there is an immediate connection with the coda (mm. 367–417). Continuous sixteenths, then triplet-eighths

8–6. Schubert, *Piano Sonata in B♭*, op. post., fourth movement

8–6. *(Continued)*

underlay the entire second theme group in the recapitulation, in contrast to the quarters and eighths that appear in the corresponding passages in the exposition.

There is a fundamental difference between these late nineteenth-century sonata forms, in which a loose construction prevails or else mandates wholesale recomposition of the recapitulation, and the earlier sonata forms, in which the construction of the exposition is designed to fulfill the necessary roles of the recapitulation. For outside of those monothematic Haydn movements in which avoiding thematic repetition requires a recomposed recapitulation, Classical movements in which the second theme group is not substantially the same in exposition and recapitulation (barring the obligatory transposition) are rare. The change of key often leads to changes in register, and other minor details may change. But the larger rhythmic-phrasing structure remains pretty much intact. The balance of continuity and conclusion is designed to work in both sections of the movement. First theme groups are commonly altered in length, in texture, in rhythm, and even in harmonic structure to create continuity from the development into the recapitulation. Often an abbreviated first theme group is followed by a short second developmental section. But second theme groups maintain the structure described earlier in this section.

Brahms is probably the only composer of the latter half of the nineteenth century who attempted to re-create a vibrant sonata form as a single overarching form for a movement. The extent to which he had to transform his ideas to achieve this goal is perhaps nowhere so clearly demonstrated as in the two versions of the *Piano Trio,* op. 8. The first version was composed in 1854, when Brahms was but twenty-one.[3] In its grandiose themes, its large layout, the inclusion of a fugato in the recapitulation, and the general freedom of structure, the first movement is an enthusiastic youthful view of the monumental middle- and late-Beethoven sonata forms, but without the unified conception of the form that Beethoven had. The individual sections bear no relation to the content of a Beethoven movement. The first theme group alternates between versions of the opening theme and subsidiary material for fifty-three measures. The second theme group is structured as a large period followed by closing phrases. But in its length, slow rhythms, and separate phrases, it emerges as a loose section following the first theme group, not as a dynamic part of the larger form. The entire second theme group is absent from the recapitulation, replaced by a fugue on a connecting idea within the second theme group, then a developmental section using first-group material. So in addition to the episodic nature of the second theme group's structure that is apparent as one listens to it, the group, in retrospect, seems more like a contrasting section in a ternary or other sectional structure than a passage whose return to the tonic is the essence of the form.

The later version of the trio was composed in 1889 for inclusion in the complete edition Simrock was preparing. Brahms' dissatisfaction with the earlier version spurred him to recompose the piece substantially. Only the scherzo remained unchanged. In the first movement, Brahms retained the structure of the opening theme group with only some instrumentation changes. The second theme group is entirely new, although it remains in G♯ minor (VI). It opens with a period whose antecedent and consequent phrases are four measures long. A contrasting section, working on motives from this theme, leads to a new beginning of the theme. But this time, the section is not phrased as a period. Instead, it leads in a single phrase to a conclusive cadence. The postcadential extensions lead either back to the opening via the first ending or into the development.

Whereas the first version features a complete return of the first theme group for the opening of the recapitulation, the second version is substantially different. The development ends with a cadence in G♯ minor (VI), paralleling the cadence that concludes the exposition. From this cadence arises the opening theme, changing the focus to B major only in midtheme. The triplet rhythms of the end of the development persist, creating continuities that cross phrasing boundaries. The whole section is much shorter than in the exposition (twenty-one measures versus fifty-three earlier), and leads directly into the second theme group. This is similar in structure to the exposition but changed in dynamics and instrumentation, creating quite a different sense of shape. The result is a single gesture to the entire movement despite its length. A simple overall tonal structure, appropriate phrasing continuities throughout the movement, and composite rhythms that cross sectional boundaries help project this structure.

RHYTHM AND STYLE

The stylistic differences between late eighteenth- and early nineteenth-century music on the one hand and later nineteenth-century music on the other are commonly described in terms of harmonic language, orchestration, types of forms and genres used, and aesthetic attitudes. Purely rhythmic distinctions also differentiate these musics from each other. The third essay in Cone's *Musical Form and Musical Performance* approaches stylistic differentiation from the perspective of rhythm. Cone's concern is mostly with the rhythmic units and metric levels that are the focus of attention in various stylistic eras. Grout, in *A History of Western Music,* notes less variety as a factor differentiating Romantic rhythms from the more varied rhythms of Classical music. Grout relates this rhythmic characteristic to the focus on lyrical melody and the resulting nature of nineteenth-century form.[4]

The present chapter suggests further avenues for exploring stylistic similarities and differences between eras on the basis of larger rhythmic shapes and processes as they affect musical forms and continuity. Consider the case of Haydn's "monothematic" sonata forms. Even many recent writers who acknowledge the inadequacy of thematic layouts as a description of sonata form present the obligatory discussion noting the special nature of those Haydn movements in which the arrival on the second key is heralded by a new statement of the opening theme. In terms of rhythm and phrasing, however, these Haydn movements agree in all essentials with the Classical sonata-form structure discussed earlier. In the first-movement exposition of Haydn's *Symphony No. 104,* for instance, the second theme group opens with a somewhat changed transposition of the sixteen-measure period that begins the *allegro* (measures 49–63, counting measure 1 as the beginning of the *allegro*). As in contemporaneous second theme groups, the cadence of the consequent phrase connects (here by means of a deceptive resolution) with the beginning of new material. An extended passage elaborates first the precadential music and then the postcadential music of the opening period of the exposition: measures 64–66 work with the syncopation figure of 13–15; measures 70–73 recall the stationary $^6_4$'s of 16–23. All of measures 64–83 is cast in a single large motion moving to the dominant (measures 76ff.) and cadencing on the tonic. This cadential arrival in measure 83 initiates the new texture of the closing material. A series of eliding phrases reiterate tonic cadences (mm. 83–96 [14 measures] eliding to 96–100 [5 measures] eliding to 100–104 [5 measures], and the final tonic pedal). And even though the second theme group in the recapitulation is substantially recomposed, the structural outline remains the same. The theme that confirms arrival in the dominant in the exposition may be the opening theme. But its rhetoric, phrasing, and rhythmic continuity are that of the late eighteenth-century sonata form.

A musical form is an outgrowth of the inner dynamic of the musical compositions in which it arises. The structuring of that form—the relation between form and content—is altered when the stylistic dynamic is changed. Sonata form from Haydn through Beethoven, for instance, is a dramatic form—a form in which the themes and motives exist to play a role in the whole. It is significant that descriptions of the form by Haydn's, Mozart's, and Beethoven's contemporaries concentrate on the large periods and the tonal structure, not on thematic layout. Only after Beethoven's death did a new generation of musicians enshrine the theme as the essence of the form. The theorists of the late eighteenth century who did not emphasize themes in their descriptions of the form reflected an emphasis on the vibrant rhetorical basis of the music they were describing. Similarly, the nineteenth-century theorists for whom sonata form became a thematic process reflected a music in which thematic contrast had indeed become the essence of the form.

9

RHYTHM AND POLYPHONY

Rhythmic aspects of polyphony include a number of issues. We have already discussed one of these aspects, composite rhythm,[1] in several chapters as it concerns the projection of changing levels of activity, the articulation of or continuity across sectional divisions (whether they are phrases or larger units), and stylistic differentiation.

Another important aspect of rhythm, one that has not received much attention in recent writings on rhythm, concerns the rhythmic differentiation of the individual parts in a texture. This is of importance to both the foreground texture of polyphonic and relatively homophonic textures as well as to the structural polyphony that underlies all tonal music. The first section of this chapter discusses rhythmic differentiation of parts in foreground textures; the second section extends this discussion to structural polyphony. The latter discussion relates rhythmic differentiation in structural polyphony to continuity in phrase rhythm as demonstrated in earlier chapters. Finally, the chapter concludes by illustrating the relationship between such structural continuities and the form of polyphonic compositions such as fugues.

RHYTHMIC DIFFERENTIATION OF PARTS IN A TEXTURE

The importance of independent rhythmic profiles to help project the independence of separate voices in a texture has long been a concern of composition and counterpoint manuals, even where they did not address the topic directly. Johann Fux, for instance, does not set aside a separate division for this discussion in his classic composition treatise *Gradus ad parnassum* (Vienna, 1725). But he does close the discussion of fugue in three parts by recommending the "use of tied notes in one or another part as often as it is possible. It is astonishing how much advantage can be gained through this device throughout the course of the composition, since almost every part is distinguished from the others in its movement and becomes thus more easily comprehensible. *This consideration holds not only here but in any style of composition.*"[2] Indeed, the importance of rhythmic variety among the components of a texture is just as essential to their independence as the use of oblique or contrary motion. And it is as important to relatively homophonic textures as it is to polyphonic ones. Melodies with rapid notes—perpetual motions or passage work—more often than not stand out by having an accompaniment that moves quite a bit slower than the melody. Slower, more lyrical melodies more often than not have relatively active patterned accompaniments.

But it is of course in polyphonic textures that rhythmic differentiation of voices is particularly crucial to their independence. This is true of a simple piece, such as Bach's *Two-Part Invention in C Major* (in which sixteenths in one part are often counterpointed by eighths in the other), of nearly any fugue subject and its countersubject, and of the separate subjects of a double or triple fugue (such as the *Fugue in C♯ Minor, Well-Tempered Clavier*, I). Yet rhythmic differentiation of voices often serves more than the relatively decorative function of projecting their independence. Cooper and Meyer draw attention to the role of a fugal countersubject in clarifying the rhythm (for them, the grouping) and meter of the subject itself, citing the subjects from the F♯-minor and A-major fugues from the *Well-Tempered Clavier*, II[3] (see example 9-1). In our terminology, the countersubject of the *F♯-minor Fugue* provides durational accents that coincide with points of harmonic change to make it clear that the long notes in the subject are syncopations. In the *A-Major Fugue*, it is not until the entry of the third voice that durational and harmonic-change accents coincide convincingly.

The manner in which the rhythm of a fugal countersubject clarifies and complements the subject parallels the way subject and countersubject complement each other in terms of voice leading. Since a fugue subject stands alone at the opening of the fugue, it must make linear, melodic, and rhythmic sense on its own. At the same time, it must allow for and even invite the complementary voice leadings and rhythms of the counterpoints that will join it. Recognition of the voice-leading, rhythmic, and sometimes motivic

Bach, *Fugue in F♯ Minor (Well-Tempered Clavier*, II)

Bach, *Fugue in A Major* (Well-Tempered Clavier, II)

9–1

complementarism of subject and countersubject can assist both in the appreciation of existing fugues and in the pedagogy of composing such passages.

The opening of the *Fugue in G Minor (Well-Tempered Clavier,* I) is representative, not so much for the specifics of the interaction (for no two Bach fugues are quite alike), but for the principles involved. Example 9-2 presents the subject. The antecedent and consequent segments of the subject are sharply differentiated in motives, rhythms, and voice leading. Conspicuously missing from the antecedent part is the third of the tonic chord, allowing for the powerful arrival on scale-step 3 at the end of the subject. The conse-

9–2. Bach, *Fugue in G Minor (Well-Tempered Clavier,* I)

quent segment suggests a dominant-to-tonic progression, with the absence of the leading tone progressing to the tonic and any continuation of scale-step 6 left hanging in the antecedent.

The countersubject picks up the loose ends in the voice leading and relates the two halves in terms of motive and rhythm (see example 9-3). Scale-step 3 (now in D minor) is a goal in the first part of the countersubject, the leading tone-to-tonic voice leading ends the countersubject, and hanging scale-step 6 in the subject (measure 2, beat 4) is picked up in the countersubject. The countersubject introduces the rhythm of the consequent part of the subject to fill in the rhythmically inactive midsubject. The rhythm of the antecedent of the subject ends the countersubject: ⁊ ♪♪♩ | ♩ . The motivic inversions noted in example 9-4 intensify the relationship between subject and countersubject and even call attention to the implied inversion that opens the subject itself: D-E♭, G-F♯.

9–3. Bach, *Fugue in G Minor* (*Well-Tempered Clavier*, I)

9–4

In the music of a composer like Bach, whose musical language is so deeply rooted in counterpoint, exchange among the components of a texture even characterizes much of his homophonic music. The opening ritornello of the *Brandenburg Concerto No. 2* is a case in point (example 9-5). The first-violin part is such a complete and well-shaped melody by itself that the passage is easily heard as homophonic. Registrally, the melody establishes its middle range and then proceeds to explore the upper register (measures 3–4) and then the lower (measures 5–6), reaching its peak immediately before ending on its opening pitch. Rhythmically, the repeated measures that open the melody (1–2, 3–4, 5–6) change to repeated half measures in measure 7. Complementing this increased pace of motivic activity and the registral sweep is an acceleration in the essential harmonic rhythm leading to the cadence in measure 8.

Supporting this melody is a texture containing three rhythmic components that circulate throughout the texture: *a,* the continuous sixteenths; *b,* the mixture of eighths and pairs of sixteenths that opens the melody; and *c,* the brass fanfares of the opening.

measures:	1–2	3–4	5–6	7	8
brass:	c	——	c	——	b
fl., ob., upper str.:	b	a	b	a	——
bass:	a	c	c	c	c

Each component of the texture has its own rhythmic profile, just as if the piece were a three-part invention. Among innumerable other excerpts by Bach that illustrate such rhythmic polyphony, the opening choruses of the St. John and St. Matthew passions dramatically illustrate Bach's capacity for handling three, four, and even five rhythmically differentiated components in textures that are not fugal.

Whereas Bach maintains polyphonic rhythms even in relatively homophonic textures, many a nineteenth-century fugato lapses into homophony shortly after or even during the fugal exposition because of the failure of the separate contrapuntal parts to maintain individual profiles. The fugatos in Schubert's *Wanderer Fantasy,* op. 15 (fourth movement) or Saint-Saëns' *Danse Macabre* (measures 138ff.) are two obvious instances. In general (though with exceptions), nineteenth-century music features separate rhythmic profiles for textural components. But rhythms in each component tend not to change so often and there is less give-and-take between the rhythms of the individual components.

Homorhythmic Textures. The opposite of a polyrhythmic texture, where separate components each have their own rhythms is a homorhythmic texture, in which all parts are in rhythmic unison. It may well be tautological to note that only in some truly homophonic textures do all voices in a texture have the same rhythmic profile. But it is revealing that such homorhythmic textures are not all that common outside of obvious chorales and tutti unisons and often occupy a striking position in a work. This is true of slower rhythms as well as faster ones. Think, for instance, of the dramatic chromaticism of measures 71–74 (and 212–15) in that largely diatonic first movement of Mozart's *String Quartet,* K. 458 *("The Hunt"),* set off by the striking cessation of polyrhythmic activity, of the role homorhythmic texture plays in establishing the special atmosphere of the *Heiliger Dankgesang* in Beethoven's *String Quartet,* op. 132, or of the effect of the nearly homorhythmic texture that begins the poco andante in the finale of the *"Eroica"* (measures 349ff.), after nearly one hundred measures of divergent rhythmic activity at allegro molto.

In fast movements, the convergence of all parts in a single fast

9–5. Bach, *Brandenburg Concerto No. 2,* first movement

9–5. *(Continued)*

rhythmic value often occurs at climactic points. The first movement of Mozart's *Piano Sonata*, K. 545, for instance, features continuous sixteenths in one part for much of the movement. Only in two passages, however, do both hands join in sixteenth notes for more than two notes at a time: immediately before the trill that concludes the second theme group in the exposition and at the same point in the recapitulation (see example 9-6). The more extended rhythmic unison in the recapitulation joins with the changed registral sweep of the melody to help bring the movement to its final tonic arrival. (Review the discussion in chapter 8 of the second theme group's rhythms.) The same effect can operate in larger contexts. The F-major coda (allegro, measures 133ff.) that concludes the finale of Beethoven's *String Quartet,* op. 95, draws a good part of its shim-

9–5. *(Continued)*

mering brilliance from its mostly homorhythmic eighth-note texture, especially after a movement that earlier features strikingly individual rhythmic profiles in its textural components, with only
brief bursts of rhythmic unison.

STRUCTURAL POLYPHONY

Peter Westergaard, in his 1962 article "Some Problems in Rhythmic
Theory and Analysis," notes the failure of Cooper and Meyer's
1960 study *The Rhythmic Structure of Music* (and, by extension,
other writings on rhythm prior to that date) "to consider the rhythmic structure of polyphony." He remarks that "while much tonal
music has little polyphonic interest in its surface texture, almost all

9–6. Mozart, *Piano Sonata*, K. 545, first movement

tonal music of any stature has considerable polyphonic interest in its underlying structure."[4] Westergaard's criticism remains valid for all the writings on rhythm since that date. Virtually all the music examples discussed in studies on rhythm are homophonic. Even where the excerpts feature a polyphonic texture, the discussion concerns only a single part. Except for the Cooper and Meyer fugal examples discussed earlier in this chapter and a single analysis by Berry demonstrating cross-metric placements in Brahms' *Horn Trio*, op. 40,[5] hardly any comments even relate to foreground polyphony.

I believe that the root of the problem is the general insistence by writers on rhythm that a phrase must project only a single accentual profile and that the task of the analyst is to find that one profile. Perhaps the most straightforward statement of this position appears in Schenker's analysis in *Free Composition* of the opening of the *Fugue in C♯ Minor, Well-Tempered Clavier*, I. Schenker intends to demonstrate the difficulty of applying a hypermeter to a fugal texture (see example 9-7). Schenker despairs at the prospect of the

9–7. Schenker, *Free Composition*, fig. 149/8a

252

continual reinterpretations that would be necessary if a hypermeter were to be applied to this as well as to many other polyphonic contexts.

As long as musical content moved principally in imitations of canonic and fugal forms, it was somehow illogical to presuppose a specific metric scheme. Each of the numerous imitations, after all, involved reinterpretation [of the placement of metric accents]. Where would we find ourselves if we were to pursue the idea of reinterpretation in the manner indicated at a)? . . . Only the freeing of music from too much imitation allowed rhythm and meter to interact in a way that might serve absolute diminution.[6]

Let us pass over Schenker's too well known historical biases as well as the assertion, remarkable for Schenker, that even J. S. Bach in the *Well-Tempered Clavier* was incapable of superseding the bane of what was for Schenker that pretonal pseudomusic. Instead, let us examine the assumption, enunciated by Schenker and implicit in other writers, that only relatively homophonic textures allow a clear projection of large-scale rhythm. This assumption is itself based on two others: first, that meter is the only form of large-scale accentuation, and second, that there is only a single large-scale accentuation to a passage. Earlier chapters in the present study have demonstrated that meter is but one form of accentuation in tonal music. In addition, there are often conflicting large-scale articulations within tonal phrases and sections, and differing structurings of individual components within a texture. Review the discussion of the five-measure phrases in the *Chorale St. Antoni,* in which the differing accompanimental and melodic phrase divisions do not coincide, creating continuity within the phrases (examples 6-14 through 6-16). Review also the discussions of the slow movement from Beethoven's *Piano Sonata,* op. 10, no. 1, (examples 6-17 through 6-20) and Chopin's *Mazurka,* op. 67, no. 3 (examples 6-11 and 6-13). In these two passages, there is a duple grouping of measures caused by melodic subdivisions. But in both, articulations in the accompaniment create entirely different (and irregular) divisions. The points where the different structures converge become powerful arrivals that would lose much of their power if all textural components contained the same subdivisions. (Review the recomposition of the Beethoven passage in example 6-20.)

As argued in chapters 6 and 7, the separate accentuations of the individual textural components are a principal factor—perhaps even the primary factor—in creating continuity within phrases and sections in tonal music. And it was possibly the promotion of this type of continuity that was the source of Fux's recommendation, cited earlier in this chapter, that different rhythmic profiles of different voices were so important in all styles of composition. The crucial word here is *continuity*. The study of a single part in a texture may well lead to a segmentation of that part into its separate structural units. But the study of all parts in a texture leads to the integration of all the multiple accentuations of all textural components into the continuity of the phrase or even the piece as a whole. For even in the most homophonic of textures, bass parts and harmonic structures often have continuities of their own—continuities and articulations that cut across those of the principal melody. Listen to the opening of Beethoven's "Spring" *Sonata*, op. 24, in example 9-8. The texture seems as homophonic as Classical textures ever are. The melody clearly subdivides into pairs of measures on the basis of the motives as well as the rests. But these melodic pairs of measures are not the only segmentations in this phrase. At least three other essential segmentations are present here. First, there are the

9–8. Beethoven, *Sonata for Violin and Piano*, op. 24, first movement

retained harmonies of measures 4–5 and 6–7 that cut right across the melodic divisions. Second, the harmonies of measures 1–8 recur at a faster pace in measures 8–10 (I, VI, II, V, I), undercutting the regularity of the two-measure melodic subdivisions. Third, there is the registral contour of the bass in measures 1–6, establishing a three-measure grouping. Listen to example 9-9. The ten-measure phrase is a single, beautifully paced entity. The separate structuring of each component, especially in the early portion of the phrase, sets the two-measure melodic segments in a continuous flow. The accelerated harmonic repetition approaching the cadence complements the return to the opening melodic register (completing the 3-2-1 structural voice leading) and the more continuous melodic rhythm to lead to the final cadence—the first point where the structuring of all components converges. As in other examples presented earlier, attempting to reduce the passage to a regular duple hypermeter would not clarify the rhythmic structure but destroy the flow of the music.

9–9

It would seem that a Schenkerian approach to tonal music, with its emphasis on counterpoint at each level, would be the best way to approach the rhythms of structural polyphony in tonal music.[7] But as applied by Schenker and most of his disciples, this approach emphasizes the manner in which accompanimental voice leadings support a primary melodic line. Such a methodology will not lead to an appreciation of the independent structures of each textural component. An understanding of the structural rhythms of tonal music requires the recognition of the structural polyphony and its requirement of independent voices—independent not only in line but in rhythm as well. Those theorists who dwell upon the rhythmic structuring of a single voice or who insist on the regularity of a single composite hypermeter lose this polyphonic perspective on musical continuity.

LARGER RHYTHMS IN POLYPHONIC GENRES

From a perspective that recognizes the structural polyphony of all tonal music, the difference between relatively polyphonic and overtly homophonic surface textures remains as a difference of degree, not a difference of kind. In highly motivic polyphony, such as in fugal textures, each part asserts its independent structure. Review the opening of Bach's *Fugue in C♯* minor in example 9-7. The entrance of each new voice on the cadential arrival of the previous entry is akin to a phrasing elision in a more homophonic texture. I attribute Schenker's discomfort with this passage not to any one of these elisionlike connections (for he accepts such elisions elsewhere) but to the prevalence of such connections in this and so many other similar textures.

Yet the elisions in this fugal exposition are simpler than many others commonly occurring in fugues. In the passage in example 9-10, not one but two voices begin before and continue right through a textural cadence. Occasionally, there are continuities so broad that it is not until the middle of a passage that a listener is aware that a new section has begun. A particularly striking instance is the E♭-major entry of the subject in Bach's *Fugue in C Minor, Well-Tempered Clavier,* I (see example 9-11). The beginning of measure 11 is a continuation of the sequence begun in measure 9—not until later in measure 11 or even in measure 12 is a listener aware that a new triple-counterpointed subject entry is under way and that the local key is E♭, not A♭ (as implied by the D♭ in measure 11 and the continually falling fifths of the previous measures).

Such overlapping continuities also characterize the larger form of many of Bach's fugues and can help unravel the continuing confusion concerning fugal form. The attempt to apply thematic formal models to fugues arose with the schools of textbook fugue writing in the nineteenth century.[8] Despite the remarkable diversity of layouts in Bach's fugues, many theorists argued for a basic three-part structure: the fugal exposition that establishes the tonic key, a middle section modulating through several keys and displaying a

9–10. Bach, *Fugue in C Major* (*Well-Tempered Clavier,* I)

9–11. Bach, *Fugue in C Minor* (*Well-Tempered Clavier,* I)

variety of contrapuntal options, and a concluding section with entries again in the tonic key. This model still appears in recent text-
books. It is beyond dispute that Baroque fugues, like virtually all
tonal pieces, begin in the tonic, move away from the tonic, and return to the tonic later in the piece. As a result, minimal evidence exists in each fugue to affirm this conception of fugal structure. But
the layout of an individual fugue often leads to quite a different
structuring.

Figure 9-1 outlines the order of entries and episodes in Bach's
Fugue in C Minor, Well-Tempered Clavier, I, along with the keys
and cadences. The tonal basis of a three-part structure crosses a
large-scale binary structure that arises from the parallel ordering of
events in measures 3–10 and 15–23. The lower brackets in figure 9-
1 illustrate these parallel sections: a statement of the fugal answer
(measures 3–4 and 15–16), the first episode (within the exposition
in measures 5–6, recurring in invertible counterpoint at the twelfth,
then reinverted at the octave in measures 17–19), a subject statement (measures 7–8 and 20–21), the second episode (measures 9–
10, recurring with upper voices exchanged and the harmonies displaced by half a measure in 22–23). This binary division (with the
second half of the piece beginning in measure 15) is itself contradicted by the placement of the cadence on G in measure 17—the
only strong cadence before the tonic cadence in measure 29 (both
cadences with a root-position V-I and a melodic arrival on the

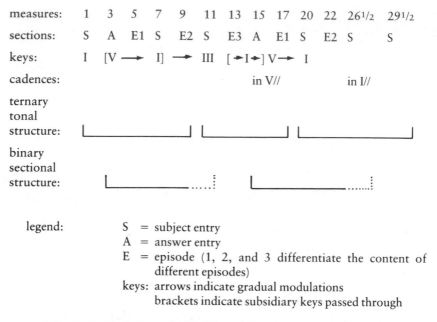

Fig. 9–1. Bach, *Fugue in C Minor:* order of entries and episodes

tonic). If this sole cadence in measure 17 is not to be merely an internal articulation within a section, it suggests a binary division in which the second part of the piece begins in measure 17, not measure 15. The point is not to choose among these possibilities, but to recognize that the piece is a single, continuous whole. Just as we have seen continuity within phrases created by overlapping continuities in independent voices or textural components, the larger continuity of this fugue arises because of overlapping sectional divisions.

Ludwig Czaczkes was apparently the first to write of the binary-structure parallelisms of this fugue. But he misses the point with his droll comment that "the form of this fugue was not properly recognized until today in the year 1956"![9] Does he really believe that for over two centuries no one recognized the true form of such a well-known piece? His slicing of the piece is no more "the" form than the partitions proposed by Riemann, Werker, Schenker, Busoni, and others before and since.[10] Each partitioning of the piece is plausible according to the criteria of its author, but none excludes the others. It is the composite of all these continuities that characterizes the piece.

The sectional overlaps of this and other Bach fugues are different from the continuities between sections of sonata-form movements that we noted in chapter 8. It is one thing to have a continuous rhythm proceeding across an otherwise clear sectional division. (Review the discussion of Beethoven's "Appassionata" *Sonata* in chapter 8.) It is quite another thing to have several sectionalizations of a piece, each of which is convincing in itself, and all of them in conflict with each other concerning the placement of sectional divisions. The only parallel with later tonal music is in the polyphony that creates continuity within phrases.

EPILOGUE

This study has explored the multiplicity of accentuations, groupings, and continuities that abound in tonal music. Freeing the concept of accent from that of beat establishes accentuation and meter
as separate, yet overlapping categories. Freeing the notion of meter
from a single level to a range of levels opens up for examination the
wide range of metric interactions that occurs in the repertoire. Separating the notion of hypermeter from the variety of larger accentuations, groupings, and continuities that occur in single voices and in
textural components opens up whole panoramas of large-scale
rhythms.

Such a perspective yields insights for the analyst, the listener,
and the performer. For the analyst, the most obvious advantage is
the clarification that results from separating concepts that are related but not identical. Metric accent, for instance, is indeed a type
of accentuation; and several types of accentuation do indeed frequently occur on points of metric accent in much tonal music. But
metric accent is not the only type of accentuation. A separation of
these concepts opens up for exploration such diverse issues as the
role of accentuation in creating continuity—indeed, in creating musical interest—and in creating stylistic differences.

Recognizing the multiplicity of rhythms makes a listener
aware of the seemingly endless novelties that can be discovered in
pieces the better one gets to know them. The more overt rhythms,
often the more regular patternings, will often be perceived first. As
these become more familiar, other accentuations, especially those
that require an anticipation of now-expected events, can come into
focus. Fresh performances of a piece, live or recorded, inevitably
emphasize different accentuations and continuities, opening yet
further shapings. This effect is part of the reason that a single re-
cording of a work, no matter how ideal it may seem after one or

several hearings, inevitably becomes irksome; once fully learned, its ever-identical accentuations and continuities that once opened new vistas within the piece now preclude further ones.

In the sense that any piece contains immeasurably large numbers of rhythmic shapings of details and of larger shapes, no single performance can ever hope to project them all. Recognizing the factors that create these shapes and the sometimes contradictory results that proceed from projecting them opens avenues of exploration for performers.

This approach of multiple rhythms also bears on the psychology of hearing. One current approach to musical perception argues that as we hear a composition, we continually compare the actual events of the piece with our expectations based on our knowledge of and experience with the style and the individual piece.[1] Such an approach suggests growing boredom with the piece on repeated hearings. Our expectations will come ever closer to the actual events in the piece as we become more familiar with the piece, reducing that dynamic interaction between expectation and perception. This does not accord with our experience of growing interest in a great piece the better we know it. The present work suggests a rather different perspective. Only as we become more familiar with a piece do we move beyond relatively superficial features and become cognizant of evermore intricate rhythmic structures—and, hence, of the structurings of the aspects that create these rhythms. Becoming aware of these structurings, both of details and of larger features, is what makes the piece more and more interesting as we learn to expect each of its events.

In Pursuit of the One Analysis

One of the most tempting fallacies of any discussion about music—whether formal or informal—is to generalize a particular viewpoint into a universal law. As we theorists have become evermore adept at understanding the role of harmonies and of harmonic-melodic interactions (structural voice leading), it has become ever easier to assume that it is in this sphere that the essential structure of a piece is to be found. But this sphere, no matter how central its role, is but one dimension of tonal music. This is so even if we leave aside the roles of texture, themes, dynamics, timbre, and so forth, and restrict our attention to purely pitch factors. Motivic relations among

261

harmonies—both functional harmonies and nonharmonic-tone collections—and the structure of simultaneities directly affect our hearing and may well be a primary factor in our ability to differentiate one composer from another.[2] Our inability thus far to develop a formal way of dealing with these aspects does not diminish their importance to a piece.

In the rhythmic sphere, much attention has been paid to the nature of meter. Cooper and Meyer, for instance, define accent in terms of strong beats. Yeston uses stratifications to lead to metric groupings. Komar's generative approach is based on pairing pitch structures with metric positions at many levels. Schachter too extends meter to higher structural levels. It is undeniable that meter is a crucial feature of tonal music. The sense of arrival is a crucial feature of tonal music. The sense of arrival on a primary harmony, for instance, is usually a product of metric position as well as of purely pitch factors. But metric accents are not the only form of accentuation. At and below the primary metric level, other accentuations, often out of synchronization with the meter, promote continuity. As demonstrated in several recomposed excerpts during the course of this book, removing these cross-accentuations transforms many an imaginative passage into a plodding, thumping one. At higher levels, it is often possible to organize the music into one or more levels of hypermeter. But doing so represses other accentuations and overlooks other continuities—accentuations and continuities that often are the lifeblood of the piece.

In sum, just as no one pitch aspect is "the" pitch structure of a piece, no one rhythmic aspect—be it meter, accent, level of activity, or any other—is "the" rhythm of that piece. Especially at our current state of understanding rhythm, limiting our focus to one or two aspects as the only important ones and insisting on one way to organize a passage, whether for performing or hearing, will stymie us in improving our understanding of the passage. Only by exploring the many aspects of rhythm and their interactions will we continue to widen our understanding of the rhythms of tonal music.

NOTES
INDEX OF MUSICAL EXAMPLES
GENERAL INDEX

NOTES

1. The Study of Rhythm

1. Edward T. Cone, *Musical Form and Musical Performance* (New York: W. W. Norton, 1968), pp. 32–34.

2. Charles J. Smith, "Rhythm Restratified," *Perspectives of New Music* 16 (1977): 145.

3. Grosvenor Cooper and Leonard Meyer, *The Rhythmic Structure of Music* (Chicago: Univ. of Chicago Press, 1960).

4. Cone, *Musical Form.*

5. Arthur Komar, *A Theory of Suspensions* (Princeton: Princeton Univ. Press, 1971). A second edition (1979) is available from Peer Publications, 5600 Ridge Oak Drive, Austin, Texas, 78731.

6. Maury Yeston, *The Stratification of Musical Rhythm* (New Haven: Yale Univ. Press, 1976).

7. Peter Westergaard, *An Introduction to Tonal Theory,* part 3 (New York: W. W. Norton, 1975).

8. "Rhythm and Linear Analysis: A Preliminary Study," *Music Forum* 4 (1976): 281–334; "Rhythm and Linear Analysis: Durational Reduction," *Music Forum* 5 (1980): 197–232.

9. Wallace Berry, *Structural Functions in Music* (Englewood Cliffs: Prentice-Hall, 1976), chapter 3.

10. John Graziano, "A Theory of Accent in Tonal Music of the Classic-Romantic Period" (unpubl. diss., Yale University, 1975).

11. Berry, *Structural Functions,* p. 30.

12. Benjamin Boretz, "In Quest of the Rhythmic Genius," *Perspectives of New Music* 9/2 and 10/1 (1971): 154.

13. Cooper and Meyer, *Rhythmic Structure,* p. 6.

14. Berry, *Structural Functions,* contains extensive discussions of textural and rhythmic activity in chapters 2 and 3 (pp. 184–424).

2. Accent

1. Cooper and Meyer, *Rhythmic Structure,* p. 8. Roger Sessions makes the same point in *Harmonic Practice* (New York: Harcourt, Brace & World, 1951), p. 83.

2. Cooper and Meyer, *Rhythmic Structure.* In adopting poetic feet, Cooper and Meyer follow a number of earlier writers, among them Rudolph Westphal in

265

Allgemeine Theorie der Musikalischen Rhythmik (Leipzig: Breitkopf & Härtel, 1880); Hugo Riemann in *System der Musikalischen Rhythmik und Metrik* (Leipzig: Breitkopf & Härtel, 1903); and James Mursell in *The Psychology of Music* (New York: W. W. Norton, 1937).

3. Cone, *Musical Form*, pp. 27–31, *passim*.

4. See Komar, *Suspensions*, pp. 5–6, for a critique similar to that offered here.

5. Berry, *Structural Functions*, p. 335.

6. Cooper and Meyer, *Rhythmic Structure*, pp. 99ff.

7. Berry, *Structural Functions*, on pages 324–26 renotates the opening of the slow movement of Mozart's "Jupiter" *Symphony*, K. 551. See the discussion of this passage in chapter 3 of the present study. Komar, *Suspensions*, example 156 (p. 118), suggests a relocation of the barlines at the opening of the slow movement of Beethoven's *Piano Sonata*, op. 7. Arnold Schoenberg's rebarring of a theme from Mozart's *Piano Quartet*, K. 478, has received considerable attention. See notes 7–9 in chapter 3 for references to Schoenberg's analysis and other commentaries.

8. John Graziano, "A Theory of Accent."

9. Roger Sessions, in *Harmonic Practice*, maintains that "accent means contrast, and vice versa" (p. 83). Anne Alexandra Pierce, in her dissertation "The Analysis of Rhythm in Tonal Music" (Brandeis University, 1968) defines the term similarly: "Change results in a stress, or accent. The weakest conceivable accent results from the repetition of an identical pitch with no change in any other element; the re-articulation of an identical pitch is sufficient to differentiate it from the note preceding and thus create a change, and any distinguishable change results in an accent, no matter how slight a one" (p. 25). These definitions, similar to the one given here, differ on two crucial points: they do not specify the location of the accent caused by change or contrast, and they do not specify the location of the unaccented state with which the accent contrasts. In the case of a repeated note, Pierce's argument suggests that the second note is accented in relation to the first. This would lead to ever-stronger accents in a string of repeated notes, or in nearly any passage. To avoid this problem, it is essential to specify that accent is a phenomenon that marks a beginning and contrasts with the unaccented state of a preceding or following continuation or silence.

10. Robert Cogan and Pozzi Escot argue that longer notes are often accented "because of the greater energy required to launch a long note than a short one." See *Sonic Design* (Englewood Cliffs: Prentice-Hall, 1976), pp. 232–33. The accentuation on a long note is a quality inherent in the note, not one added on the volition of the performer. Indeed, in many contexts a performer will expend more energy on shorter notes to ensure their clear articulation and projection. Think of the opening of Beethoven's *Sonata for Violin and Piano*, op. 30, no. 2:

Allegro con brio

If a violinist launches the G and C "with more energy" than the sixteenths, the fast notes will be garbled.

11. This *Lied,* and indeed the entirety of *Dichterliebe,* is a marvelous resource for studying texture, its small and large-scale changes, and the interaction of texture, other musical facets, and the text. The harmonic and tonal ambiguity of *Im wunderschönen Monat Mai* (song 1) is paralleled throughout by the separate attacks and evaporating cadences of example 2-24. When the tonality settles in A major in *Aus meinen Thränen* (song 2), the texture shifts to unified attacks.

12. Graziano, "A Theory of Accent," p. 9.

13. Graziano, "A Theory of Accent," p. 23.

14. Graziano, "A Theory of Accent," pp. 104–12.

15. William Caplin, "Tonal Function and Metrical Accent: A Historical Perspective," *Music Theory Spectrum* 5 (1983): 1–14.

16. Berry, *Structural Functions,* p. 330.

17. See Graziano, "A Theory of Accent," p. 104, and virtually any harmony or counterpoint text.

18. Carl Schachter, "Rhythm and Linear Analysis," pp. 314–315; and Victor Zuckerkandl, *Sound and Symbol,* trans. Willard Trask (New York: Pantheon, 1956), pp. 100–104.

19. Cooper and Meyer link the concept of accent to that of beat, thereby losing the possibility of critically investigating either: ". . . while such factors as duration, intensity, melodic contour, regularity, and so forth obviously play a part in creating an impression of accent, none of them appears to be an invariable and necessary concomitant of accent [read: beat]." *Rythmic Structure,* p. 7.

3. Meter

1. Two distinct meanings of the term *compound meter* are current. For some writers, a compound meter is any meter containing more than three beats to the measure, including $\frac{4}{4}, \frac{4}{8}, \frac{6}{4}, \frac{9}{8}, \frac{5}{4}$, and so forth. See, for instance, William Mitchell, *Elementary Harmony,* 3rd ed. (Englewood Cliffs: Prentice-Hall, 1965), p. 19. "The duple and triple units of simple meters may be combined or compounded to form longer meters of four or more pulses." For other writers, compound meters are those in which the beat is divided into three parts. See, for instance, Allen Forte, *Tonal Harmony in Concept and Practice,* 3rd ed. (New York: Holt, Rinehart & Winston, 1979), p. 25, who describes the term as follows: "*Compound meter*: a triplet subdivision superimposed upon a simple meter."

This study prefers the first of these definitions. According to this usage, simple meters indicate one level of grouping, and compound meters indicate two or more levels.

2. The term *hemiola* (originally the Greek *hemiolia,* equivalent to the Latin *sesquialtera*) is the last remaining relic of a host of such proportional terms used to describe changing metric groupings in Renaissance mensural notation. It refers exclusively to the change from grouping of 3 + 3 to 2 + 2 + 2. Recently, the term has been improperly used to describe the reverse change. See, for instance, Allen Forte, *Tonal Harmony,* p. 427, and Maury Yeston, *Stratification,* p. 89. For an explanation of the term in mensural notation, see Willi Apel, *The Notation of Polyphonic Music,* 5th ed. (Cambridge, MA: Mediaeval Academy of America, 1953), pp. 131, 158, and 348.

3. When a subdivision is a smaller fraction of a longer value, and there is neither a previous pulse nor another intermediate value in the passage, it is often

difficult to ascertain the precise value of the subdivision. Think of French overtures, in which performers routinely double-dot the rhythm so that short values are one seventh the length of longer ones (♩·· ♪). With irregularities and rubatos, it is nearly impossible to ascertain the pulse rate of the shorter value accurately.

4. Compare Peter Westergaard's comments regarding this passage in *An Introduction to Tonal Theory,* p. 316.

5. Edward Lowinsky, in comparing Mozart's rhythms to those of his lesser contemporaries, makes somewhat similar comments about what he calls symmetries and irregularities in Mozart's rhythms. Lowinsky argues that in terms of meter, it is the presence of the irregularities (nonmetric accentuations) that gives Mozart's music its grace, in contrast to the sometimes plodding rhythms of C. P. E. Bach, Dittersdorf, and others. See "On Mozart's Rhythm," *Musical Quarterly* 42 (1956): 162–86.

Some of Lowinsky's comments, especially those about motivic continuity and development, are specific to Mozart's music. Many other positive traits that he identifies are characteristic not only of Mozart's music, but of music by most composers of interest. As demonstrated by the remaining examples in this section, as well as by discussions throughout later chapters, accentuations and continuities that cross metric boundaries on a variety of levels abound in most music by the masters.

6. See Heinrich Schenker, "Beethoven V Sinfonie," *Der Tonwille,* I (1921); the portion on the first movement is translated into English by Elliot Forbes in the Norton Critical Scores edition of the *Fifth* (1971); and Andrew Imbrie, " 'Extra' Measures and Metrical Ambiguity in Beethoven," in *Beethoven Studies,* ed. Alan Tyson (New York: W. W. Norton, 1973), pp. 55–66. For Robert P. Morgan's comments on these analyses, see "The Theory and Analysis of Tonal Rhythm," *Musical Quarterly* 64 (1978): 460–71.

7. Reprinted in *Style and Idea,* ed. Leonard Stein (New York: St. Martins Press, 1975), pp. 436–37.

8. Edward T. Cone, "Communication," *Perspectives of New Music* 1/2 (1963): 206–210.

9. Hans Keller, "Principles of Composition (II)," *The Score,* no. 27 (1960): 11; William Mitchell, "Communication," *Perspectives of New Music,* 1/2 (1963): 210–11; Maury Yeston, *Stratification,* pp. 130–39. Only Gary Wittlich, in his review of Yeston (*Journal of Music Theory* 21/2 (1977): 369–70), calls attention to the context of the passage.

10. Differing views concerning the establishment of meter have been offered by other recent theorists. They are surveyed elsewhere in the present study: see the discussions of examples 4–29 through 4–34 for comments on Yeston, and chapter 7 for a discussion of Komar, Schachter, and Westergaard (as well as comments on Schenker).

4. Metric Ambiguity and Change

1. Cooper and Meyer, *Rhythmic Structure,* pp. 89–92; Wallace Berry, *Structural Functions,* pp. 324–26.

2. For Cooper and Meyer, *accent* in this context means *strong beat.* Review pages 15–16 of the present study.

3. Maury Yeston, in *The Stratification of Musical Rhythm,* holds the same position as Cooper and Meyer concerning the establishment of meter. See the discussion of meter in a Bach prelude later in this chapter.

4. Marcel Proust, *Within a Budding Grove,* trans. C. K. Scott Moncrieff (New York: Vintage Books, 1970), pp. 76–77.

5. Lewis Lockwood shows the importance of successive changes in triplet and sixteenth figuration during Beethoven's composition process in his study on "The Autograph of the First Movement of Beethoven's Sonata for Violoncello and Pianoforte, Opus 69," *The Music Forum* 2 (1970): 1–109.

6. The changing meters and conflicting simultaneous meter signatures in different voices in a texture that appear in fugues by Reicha (published in 1805) are distinctly experimental in nature. See Antonín Rejcha, *36 Fugues for the Piano,* op. 36, ed. Václav Jan Sýkora (Kassel: Bärenreiter, 1973), especially numbers 20, 24, 28, and 30.

7. Measures 70–82 of the scherzo of Beethoven's *String Quartet,* op. 127, feature changing meter signatures. This passage is exceptional, although not unique.

8. Cooper and Meyer, *Rhythmic Structure,* p. 69.

9. Cooper and Meyer, *Rhythmic Structure,* p. 42.

10. Yeston, *Stratification.* The exposition of meter and analysis of this excerpt covers pages 65–71. Footnote 9 on page 69 discusses Cooper and Meyer's definition of meter and analysis of this excerpt. Yeston fails to see that Cooper and Meyer's definition of meter ("Meter is the *measurement* of the number of pulses between more or less regularly recurring accents," [emphasis added], p. 4) is essentially equivalent to his own. And he criticizes Cooper and Meyer for noting that F and A on beats 2 and 3 of measure 1 in the Bach prelude are unaccented—he correctly asserts that they must be accented in order to meet the demand for beats in the notated $\frac{3}{4}$ meter. But he apparently fails to recognize that accent is a relative state—the F and A are *unaccented* in relation to beat 1 of each measure, but they are *accented* in relation to the yet lower, weak eighths of each beat. Cooper and Meyer's example makes this clear.

11. Charles Smith, "Rhythm Restratified," pp. 144–76. The comments on this prelude are on pages 156–62.

12. The half-barlines after measures 1 and 3 appear in a number of Bach scores of movements in $\frac{3}{8}$ meter, apparently to show the pairing of measures. Perhaps Bach associated $\frac{3}{8}$, but not $\frac{6}{8}$, with the desired tempo. (Compare the discussion of the finale of Mozart's *Violin Concerto,* K. 216, on pages 120–121.) For another Bach movement with this notation, see the three-part *Invention in A Minor,* reprinted in facsimile in the *Clavier-Büchlein vor Wilhelm Friedemann Bach,* ed. Ralph Kirkpatrick (New Haven: Yale Univ. Press, 1959), pp. 128–29.

5. Multiple Metric Levels and Style

1. Cone, *Musical Form,* pp. 57–71.

2. Robert Cogan and Pozzi Escot, *Sonic Design* (Englewood Cliffs, NJ: Prentice-Hall, 1976), pp. 258–61.

3. Contrast the more rapid level of harmonic motion in this fugue with the E♭-G♯-B-G♮ "chord" *("Akkord")* that Arnold Schoenberg gathers from a weak-

beat nonharmonic-tone collection in measure 152 of the first movement of Mozart's *Fortieth*. When Schoenberg proceeds to build an entire progression out of this chord, noting that "one cannot hold anything against it—after all it's by Mozart!" *("Dagegen kann man doch nichts haben, das ist ja von Mozart!"),* we have every right to complain that his citation is out-of-context stylistically. Mozart's "chord" functions solely as a nonharmonic-tone collection. See example 305a in Schoenberg's *Harmonielehre,* 3rd ed. (Vienna: Universal-Edition, 1922), p. 442.

4. See Howard Shanet, "Why Did Bach Transpose His Arrangements?" *Musical Quarterly* 36(1950): 180–203.

5. Cone, *Musical Form,* pp. 63–65.

6. "Im alten Marschtempo (Allegro Moderato), ohne Rücksicht auf Cello und Bässe."

7. "Celli and Bässe im Tempo fort ohne Rücksicht auf die Kl. Trommeln, welche das erste gemässigte Marschtempo beginnen."

8. Cone, *Musical Form,* pp. 57–71. Although Cone argues that this is true of High Baroque music in general, all his Baroque examples are by Bach.

9. Note the emphasis on pre-Classic vocal music as one of the historical roots of sonata form in Charles Rosen's *Sonata Forms* (New York: W. W. Norton, 1980).

10. Donald Francis Tovey, "Prefaces to Classical Concerto Cadenzas," in *The Main Stream of Music and Other Essays* (Cleveland: World Publishing, 1959), pp. 323–24.

6. Hypermeter, Meter, and Phrase Rhythms

1. Heinrich Schenker, *Free Composition,* trans. Ernst Oster (New York: Longman, 1979), par. 295, fig. 146/5. (Citations to *Free Composition [Der Freie Satz]* are to paragraph numbers to allow easy reference in both the English and German editions. All translations below are from the Oster edition.)

2. Schenker, *Free Composition,* par. 288. See also the discussion below.

3. Schenker, *Free Composition,* par. 297 and fig. 148/1.

4. Schenker, *Free Composition,* par. 297 and fig. 148/2.

5. Cone, *Musical Form,* p. 40.

6. Carl Schachter, "Rhythm and Linear Analysis, Durational Reduction," *Music Forum* 5 (1980); 205.

7. Schenker, *Free Composition,* par. 288.

8. Berry, *Structural Functions,* p. 330.

9. Berry, *Structural Functions,* pp. 330, 331, 352.

10. Leonard Meyer, *Emotion and Meaning in Music* (Chicago: Univ. of Chicago Press, 1956), pp. 109–10.

11. For Schenker's analysis see *Free Composition,* fig. 157. For Edward Cone's discussion, see *Musical Form and Musical Performance,* pp. 29–30. See also Joel Lester, "Articulation of Tonal Structures as a Criterion for Analytic Choices," *Music Theory Spectrum* 1 (1979): 73–79. Robert P. Morgan also comments on the equilibrium of afterbeat and upbeat factors in this phrase in "The Theory and Analysis of Tonal Rhythm," *Musical Quarterly* 64 (1978): 449. His discussion of this phrase covers pages 445–51.

12. See Schenker's comments in par. 286 of *Free Composition* concerning

the excerpts in fig. 137 for several remarks linking phrase unity to the unfolding of a linear span.

13. Deryck Cooke, *The New Grove*, vol. 3, (1980), 366.

14. Andrew Imbrie, " 'Extra' Measures and Metrical Ambiguity in Beethoven," in *Beethoven Studies*, ed. Alan Tyson (New York: W. W. Norton, 1973), p. 48. See also Roger Sessions, *The Musical Experience* (Princeton: Princeton Univ. Press, 1950), pp. 11–15; Cone, *Musical Form*, pp. 25–31, *passim*; and Robert Morgan, "Theory and Analysis," p. 440.

15. Schenker, *Free Composition*, par. 288. Schenker is not entirely consistent in analyzing cadences as unaccented. See the two cadences he analyzes as strong, on the beginnings of "measure groups," in example 6-1.

16. Berry, *Structural Functions*, pp. 323–24. Berry's italics.

17. Berry, *Structural Functions*, p. 2.

18. Berry, *Structural Functions*, p. 331.

19. Berry, *Structural Functions*, p. 328.

20. Sessions, *Musical Experience*, pp. 12–13.

21. The absence of a dynamic indication in the piano in measure 75 should not be construed as a factor affecting the accentuation of the phrase. With the sole exception of "p" in measure 228 of the first movement, Mozart notated not a single dynamic in any of the solo passages of this concerto. See the *Neue Mozart Ausgabe*, series 5, *Werkgruppe* 15, vol. 7, reprinted in pocket score by Bärenreiter (Bärenreiter Ausgabe 4742) and reprinted in the Norton Critical Scores (1970).

22. Schachter, "Rhythm and Linear Analysis," p. 227.

23. Arthur Komar, *Theory of Suspensions*, p. 125. Significantly, Schachter and Komar cite these syncopated $^6_4$'s only at a hypermetric level, where the nature of the hypermeter is a matter of dispute· in a four-measure phrase. I know of no passage in the tonal repertoire in which a cadential $^6_4$ enters on the second quarter of a $^4_4$ measure and resolves on the third quarter.

24. Current scholarship casts considerable doubt on Haydn's authorship of this theme. For references to relevant research, see the Norton Critical Scores edition of the Brahms *Variations on a Theme by Haydn*, op. 56, ed. Donald McCorkle (New York: W. W. Norton, 1976), pp. 28–30.

25. Schenker, *Free Composition*, par. 287.

26. Schenker, *Free Composition*, par. 288.

27. Cone, *Musical Form*, pp. 79–80.

28. Schenker, *Free Composition*, par. 286.

29. The relevant passages are in English in Oliver Strunk, *Source Readings in Music History* (New York: W. W. Norton, 1950), pp. 172–79 (Jean de Muris) and 180–90 (Jacob of Liège).

30. Schachter, "Rhythm and Linear Analysis," p. 205. He declines to defend this proposition.

31. Berry, *Structural Functions*, p. 324.

32. *Cf.* Sessions, *Musical Experience*, p. 13.

7. Rhythm and Linear Analysis

1. Heinrich Schenker, *"Das Organische der Fuge," Das Meisterwerk in der Musik* 2 (1926): 57–95. The analysis of the subject appears on pages 60–62.

This analysis is translated into English in Maury Yeston's *The Stratification of Musical Rhythm,* pp. 59–62.

2. Heinrich Schenker, *Free Composition,* par. 290.

3. Schenker, *Free Composition,* par. 287.

4. Schenker, *Free Composition,* par. 297.

5. Schenker, *Free Composition,* par. 297.

6. Benjamin Boretz, "In Quest of the Rhythmic Genius," pp. 149–55; Carl Schachter, "Rhythm and Linear Analysis," pp. 281–334.

7. Yeston, *Stratification.*

8. See examples 3.8, 4.5, 4.29, *passim.*

9. Especially illuminating are Yeston's comments on the first movement of Mozart's *Piano Sonata,* K. 332. Three-against-two patterns occur in several passages and at different levels before the triplets-against-eighths of the second theme group. See pages 103–8.

10. (Princeton: Princeton University Press, 1971).

11. Komar, "Theory of Suspensions," p. 67.

12. In Carl Schachter, "Rhythmic and Linear Analysis," pp. 197–232.

13. Schachter, "Rhythmic and Linear Analysis," p. 229.

14. Peter Westergaard, *An Introduction to Tonal Theory,* chapter 8.

15. Komar, "Theory of Suspensions," p. 155.

16. Robert P. Morgan also argues for beginning and ending accents in phrases in "The Theory and Analysis of Tonal Rhythm."

17. Schachter, "Rhythm and Linear Analysis," pp. 216–17.

18. Schachter, "Rhythm and Linear Analysis," p. 205.

19. Schachter, "Rhythm and Linear Analysis," pp. 219–20.

20. All of the excerpts analyzed by Schachter in his article on durational reduction clearly exhibit a primary meter above the level of the notated meter. He does not apply metric reduction to more complex and irregular passages (such as the opening of Mozart's *Piano Sonata,* K. 457, discussed in Schachter's earlier "Preliminary Study," *Music Forum* 4 (1976): 281–334.

21. Allen Forte, "Schenker's Conception of Musical Structure," *Journal of Music Theory* 3 (1959): 1–30; reprinted in *Readings in Schenker Analysis and Other Approaches,* ed. Maury Yeston (New Haven: Yale Univ. Press, 1977), pp. 3–37.

22. Forte, "Schenker's Conception," pp. 20–21 in the original article; p. 24 in the reprint.

23. Cone, *Musical Form,* p. 40.

8. Rhythm and Form

1. Arnold Schoenberg's comments in his *Fundamentals of Musical Composition,* ed. Gerald Strang and Leonard Stein (London: Faber and Faber, 1967), are among the only substantial discussions of this aspect of rhythm.

2. See Robert Cogan and Pozzi Escot, *Sonic Design,* pp. 261–64, for a discussion of activity, continuities, and sectional divisions in Bach's *Chaconne.*

3. The two versions are clearly labeled in all printed editions. Recordings are all of the second version, except for that by the Odeon Trio (Musical Heritage Society MHS 4215–4217).

4. Donald Jay Grout, *A History of Western Music,* 3rd ed. (New York: W. W. Norton, 1980), p. 559.

9. Rhythm and Polyphony

1. Hugo Riemann was apparently the first theorist to write about composite rhythm. See his *Musikalische Dynamik und Agogik* (Hamburg, 1884), chapter 9.

2. Translation by Alfred Mann in *The Study of Fugue,* 2nd ed. (New York: W. W. Norton, 1965), pp. 102–3, italics added.

3. Cooper and Meyer, *Rhythmic Structure,* pp. 162–64.

4. Peter Westergaard, "Some Problems in Rhythmic Theory and Analy- · sis," *Perspectives of New Music* 1 (1962): 183. Reprinted in *Perspectives on Contemporary Music Theory,* ed. Benjamin Boretz and Edward T. Cone (New York: W. W. Norton, 1972), p. 229.

5. Wallace Berry, *Structural Functions,* pp. 369–71.

6. Heinrich Schenker, *Free Composition,* par. 298.

7. See comment by Peter Westergaard, "Some Problems," p. 229 and Allen Forte, "Schenker's Conception," pp. 20–21, reprinted in *Readings in Schenker Analysis and Other Approaches,* p. 24.

8. See the essay that opens Alfred Mann's *The Study of Fugue,* pp. 3–72, for a survey of the history of fugal pedagogy.

9. Ludwig Czaczkes, *Analysen des Wolhtemperierten Klaviers . . . ,* I, (Vienna: Paul Kaltschmid, 1956), pp. 58–63. "Die Form dieser Fuge wurde bis heute, Anno 1956, nicht richtig erkannt."

10. Hugo Riemann, *Katechismus der Fugen-Komposition* (Leipzig: Max Hesse, 1890), pp. 11–15; Wilhelm Werker, *Studien uber die Symmetrie im Bau der Fugen und die motivische Zusammengehörigkeit der Präludien und Fugen des Wohltemperierten Klaviers von J. S. Bach,* (Leipzig, 1922); Ferruccio Busoni, *J. S. Bach Klavierwerke Busoni-Ausgabe: Das wohltemperierte Klavier,* I (New York: G. Schirmer, 1894; repr. Leipzig: Breitkopf & Härtel, ?), pp. 12–13.

Epilogue

1. See Leonard Meyer, *Emotion and Meaning in Music* (Chicago: Univ. of Chicago Press, 1956) and later works.

2. See Edward T. Cone, "Sound and Syntax: An Introduction to Schoenberg's Harmony," *Perspectives of New Music* 13 (1974): 21–40 for a discussion of simultaneity structure as a stylistic trait. See Joel Lester, "Simultaneity Structures and Harmonic Functions in Tonal Music," *In Theory Only* 5/5 (1981): 3–28, and the commentary on this article by David Lewin in *In Theory Only* 5/8 (1981): 12–13, for motivic approaches to simultaneity structures.

INDEX OF MUSICAL EXAMPLES

Index of Musical Examples

This index lists all musical examples and references to musical compositions. Page numbers in bold type refer to a musical example and its main discussion. Page numbers in roman type refer to other discussions of musical examples and references to musical compositions.

277

Index of Musical Examples

RHYTHMS OF TONAL MUSIC

GENERAL INDEX

General Index

This index includes terms and names of persons. For analysis of specific musical compositions, consult the Index of Musical Examples under the name of the composer, the composition, or the theorist.

Accent: and cadential $\frac{6}{4}$, 39, 179; causes of, 18–40; contour, 33–35; defined, 11, 12, 13–17; durational, 3–4, 18–23, 170; dynamic, 35–36, 78; harmonic-change, 21–26, 28, 170, 179, 181; and meter, 42; meter and dynamic, 64; meter and harmonic-change, 58–67; non-coordination of different types of, 22–25, 68–78, 177, 179, 180; pattern-beginning, 37–38; pitch-change, 22–25; and suspension, 40; textural, 61–63, 170, 171–77, 179; textural-change, 28–33. *See also* Meter
Activity, 8, 11, 127–45
Agogic accent. *See* Accent, durational
Apel, Willi, 267

Baroque music. *See* Style
Beat. *See* Pulse
Berry, Wallace, 4–5, 15, 16, 87–88, 252; on cadences, 169, 171, 193; on phrase rhythm, 162–63
Boretz, Benjamin, 4, 199

Cadence, 131; accentual weight of, 158–59, 164–67, 177–86, 208–14; and harmonic rhythm, 8–9
Caplin, William, 39
Classical music. *See* Style

Cogan, Robert, 128
Composite rhythm, 6–8, 26–27, 30–31, 219–20
Cone, Edward T., 4, 15, 81, 128, 140, 153, 187; on cadences, 169; on perception, 2; on phrase rhythm, 162, 209, 214, 216; on style, 243
Continuity, 6–7, 12, 28, 37, 70, 73, 164, 193–94, 253–59. *See also* Form; Phrase rhythm
Contour. *See* Accent, contour
Cooper, Grosvenor, 4, 17, 87–88, 118, 123, 253; on dynamics and accent, 14–15, 16
Czaczkes, Ludwig, 258

Donington, Robert, 13
Durational patterns, 6–11. *See also* Composite rhythm; Harmonic rhythm
Dynamics, 13–14, 16. *See also* Accent, dynamic

Elision, 169, 171, 189–90, 256
Escot, Pozzi, 128

Form, 218–43; and composite rhythm, 6–8; fugue, 256–59; sonata, 229–41; ternary, 225–29; theme and variations, 219–24
Forte, Allen, 214–15, 267
Fugue, 245–47, 256–59
Fux, Johann, 244–45, 254

Gould, Glenn, 74
Graziano, John, 4, 16, 38–39
Grouping, 5, 11–12
Grout, Donald, 242

283

Joel Lester is a well-known theorist and violinist. He is Professor of Music at City College of New York, is on the doctoral faculty of music at the CUNY Graduate Center, and was Visiting Professor of Theory at the Eastman School of Music (1977–78). His previous books and articles are on tonal theory, the history of theory, analysis, and musicological topics. He studied violin with Margaret Pardee, Ivan Galamian, and Paul Makanovitzky, and has been a member of the Naumburg Award–winning Da Capo Chamber Players since its founding in 1970. Professor Lester's concerns in recent years have focused on the connection between performance and more academic aspects of music—theory and musicology. He has given lecture-recitals on this subject at many colleges and at national and local conferences.